Eco-Friendly Families

Helen Coronato

ALPHA

A member of Penguin Group (USA) Inc.

Printed on recycled paper

ALPHA BOOKS

Published by the Penguin Group

Penguin Group (USA) Inc., 375 Hudson Street, New York, New York 10014, USA

Penguin Group (Canada), 90 Eglinton Avenue East, Suite 700, Toronto, Ontario M4P 2Y3, Canada (a division of Pearson Penguin Canada Inc.)

Penguin Books Ltd., 80 Strand, London WC2R 0RL, England

Penguin Ireland, 25 St. Stephen's Green, Dublin 2, Ireland (a division of Penguin Books Ltd.)

Penguin Group (Australia), 250 Camberwell Road, Camberwell, Victoria 3124, Australia (a division of Pearson Australia Group Pty. Ltd.)

Penguin Books India Pvt. Ltd., 11 Community Centre, Panchsheel Park, New Delhi—110 017, India

Penguin Group (NZ), 67 Apollo Drive, Rosedale, North Shore, Auckland 1311, New Zealand (a division of Pearson New Zealand Ltd.)

Penguin Books (South Africa) (Pty.) Ltd., 24 Sturdee Avenue, Rosebank, Johannesburg 2196, South Africa

Penguin Books Ltd., Registered Offices: 80 Strand, London WC2R 0RL, England

Dedicated to Heather Hopkins—Smoothie Barrister, Inappropriate Laugher, and Super Genius in Training—it is an honor to know you. Go and do great things.

Contents

Green Sites   205

Introduction

It is with great pleasure that I invite you to explore the environmentally savvy ideas and strategies in *Eco-Friendly Families*—a book that encourages families to embrace greener living by making practical changes in their everyday lives. Knowing that an eco-friendly lifestyle works best when everyone actively participates, I have designed family-focused activities to make going green a way of life that is both fun and functional.

Suggestions on taking a family's green inventory, an eco-inspired calendar that helps manage green goal setting, and a room-by-room eco-redesign will help all members of your family rethink their commitment to the environment and get on board with the ideas that make homes more eco-friendly. Fun and fresh ideas for reducing, reusing, and recycling; innovative alternatives for marking milestones and celebrating holidays; and detailed directions for making homemade recipes and concocting your own cleaning solutions make this a guide that goes beyond the basics. From helping your toddlers take their first green steps to getting your teens to green up their act, your family will be inspired to see going green as a way of life that evolves, not just a to-do checklist that ends.

This guide translates complicated global issues into straightforward language and engaging activities, making a conversation about environmental ethics as simple as watering the houseplants with rainwater, reusing back-to-school supplies, or hosting a neighborhood toy swap. Recipes and instructions for all activities are included, making this guide a valuable resource you'll look to time and time again. By appealing to children early in life, we help ensure that the next generation will become conscientious consumers, passionate naturalists, and responsible conservationists who are personal advocates for Earth. Together your family can take eco-actions that help the planet while preserving energy and saving money. With this book, you'll enjoy making memories whose effects extend far beyond your own backyard. We can all make a difference. *Eco-Friendly Families* can show you how.

Acknowledgments

I would like to thank my friend and agent Jacky Sach for her help and guidance throughout this project. Special thanks to my editor, Randy Ladenheim-Gil, for her expertise and encouragement, and Krista Hansing and Megan Douglass for their keen eye for detail. I would not be the eco-mama I am today without my friends in the Holistic Moms Network, especially Anna Tillinghast, Kira Campbell, and Kendrya Close. Warmest thanks go to Kim Bohn, Wendy DeSarno, and my in-laws, Mike and Kathy Coronato, who are all constant sources of support, and Christine Staahl, who gave me the time and peace of mind to finish this book.

When putting this project together, I called on the expert advice of many eco-entrepreneurs, especially Michele St. Andre, Delia Quigley, and Smadar English and friends of Genesis Farms. Patty and Heather Hopkins, Freddy DeYong, Megan Baird, Maggie Crann, Quinn Kennedy, Kelsey Perst, and Kayla Devaney all offered valuable input for activities. Thank you all for taking the time to talk with me. Cathleen Rafalko, Sue Corcoran, and the Bearlodge Writers have offered tremendous professional support—thank you. Many eco-friendly businesses were excited to be a part of this book, and I have acknowledged each throughout the book and in the appendix. I encourage readers to patronize these businesses and I thank you for all that you do.

And of course, to my husband, Tom, and my sons, Michael and Thomas, who are my favorite people on the planet—I am so grateful for my boys.

Taking Inventory: Getting Ready to Go Green

Once upon a time, not so long ago, I shopped, cooked, and cleaned for myself. And I don't just mean *myself*, as in, there was no one else in my *family*. I mean *myself*, as in, there was no one else in the *world*. I drove my car everywhere without ever considering my dependence on foreign oil. I drank expensive coffee in Styrofoam cups daily. Cleaning my apartment meant spraying the entire place with an all-purpose, bleach-based disinfectant that I wiped up with a roll of paper towels that I then threw into the garbage can, along with cans, bottles, and old magazines. My concerns were, well, my concerns— a selfish attitude, I now know.

Flash-forward to this weekend, and you'll find me checking labels for the USDA's organic approval, opting for green tea in my recycled thermos, and mixing one part vinegar with three parts water to clean my kitchen.

Why the change? I have two reasons: Michael and Thomas, my sons. Before I became a parent, my needs were personal comfort and cheap convenience. Then I became a mother and wanted nothing more than for my children's needs to be met. Instead of being solely focused on my own desires, I began to focus on the health and happiness of the two people I had just met. It wasn't long before it became glaringly apparent that achieving this new goal was going to take more effort and energy than I was used to.

While a well-balanced diet used to mean not spilling my morning coffee, prenatal nutrition made me take notice of what I was actually putting in my body. My doctor recommended that I eat organic, whole foods; take vitamins; exercise; and avoid medication. While researching optimum diets, I also found out that my cleaners could be hazardous to my health. So could the plastics I microwaved leftovers in. And I was supposed to drink more water—should it come from the tap or be bottled? Once I asked the first question, it was impossible not to keep asking more.

Before I knew it, I was questioning everything and everyone. And the answers were alarming. I immediately felt overwhelmed. Should we move to a smaller house? Give up our cars? Could we grow all of our own fruits and vegetables? How do you stop buying plastic?

I felt overwhelmed by information. I wanted to make all the right choices for my growing family but didn't know where to start. First, I assumed that I would have to throw out all the "wrong" things I had on hand and replace them with expensive alternatives. Then I worried that I wouldn't have the time it takes to "go green." But feeling compelled as a parent to take care of the world my children live in, I pressed on. The more I asked about the environment, the more I heard, "Which do you want to hear first: the good news or the bad news?" Because when it comes to our current state of environmental affairs, there are most definitely two sides to this story.

First, the bad news: there is an environmental crisis. Global warming, pollution, and strained natural resources are not the fodder of science fiction movies, but a reality. For quite some time, most people (myself included) simply agreed that nature should be enjoyed, but wouldn't—or couldn't—make the necessary leap to revering nature and respecting our place within it. This has led to some serious problems. Thankfully, I learned that there is good news. It is not too late to do something. And the things we can do to improve our environment aren't expensive or overwhelmingly time-consuming; in fact, there are a ton of ways to make eco-friendly changes in your home that can actually save your family money, time, and energy. The best part? While you are helping the environment, you are having fun doing so with the people who mean the most to you!

Lots of Little Ideas

I was fortunate enough to catch a weekend news segment that dramatically changed my life. An environmental expert, the featured guest, spoke passionately about the significance of each household making small but meaningful changes. The television guest explained that if every family switched from buying new paper towels to buying recycled paper towels, we could save tons of trees. Sitting there, I thought, "Well, I could try to do that." And I did. That was my turning point. If an environmental expert was recommending it and I was doing it, then, I figured, I had officially become part of the solution.

I continued to look for more doable ideas on energy, sustainability, and eco-health, and found more things I could try—things that were within my price range and time constraints. I heard about a new energy-saving lightbulb and, again, thought, "*That*, I could do." Instead of changing everything, I changed something. Before I knew it, one something had evolved into a household of somethings! As a new mother, not only was I learning to take care of my children, but I was, in essence, learning to take better care of everyone else's children, too. I started to feel connected to a bigger community. Wanting my kids to be a part of this new extended family, I even found things they could help with. Since they were the motivation for these changes in the first place, it felt natural to include them in the process. Excited about our family's changes, I began to share what worked (and what didn't) with other busy families looking to make a difference. Going green has been an exciting and entertaining venture for my family with benefits that extend beyond our own backyard, making a positive impact on our entire world. The same possibilities are available to you!

Heading Toward Greener Pastures

Chances are, your family already separates your paper and plastics, and you all try to remember to turn off the lights when you leave a room. You're now ready to take green living to the next level. Approaching greener living as a unified team with a positive mindset and proactive, specific language will help ensure that our going-green goals are implemented and accomplished. Throughout this book, I give you tips and strategies for making your current lifestyle more eco-friendly; for our family, that has been the key. If we were going to find a system of reducing, recycling, and reusing that we could stick to, it meant doing so within our financial and emotional comfort zone. We could not afford to buy all organic products at once, nor did we want to spend a hazy and humid summer without air conditioning; but we did find many ways to make environmentally friendly adjustments to our home. The changes we have made have had such positive effects on our household, we often find ourselves saying, "Why didn't we try this sooner?"

As I have young children, it was important for me to keep our environmental language simple and straightforward. Instead of launching into a complex discussion about why it's so important to make eco-conscious decisions, we came up with a quick, memorable means of staying on an earth-friendly track. We dubbed ourselves "Green Team Coronato" and reference our superhero-type status when faced with earth-friendly decisions. For instance, my son loves getting himself a tissue, but tends to pull out many more than he actually needs. When I saw this happen, I tried to tell him about waste and encouraged him to only take what he needed, only to be met with a blank stare. He needed something more concrete to attach to so I began calling out "Green Team Coronato" while putting back the tissues with him, and it made a much bigger impression. So much so that the last time we went out for pizza my son pulled one napkin out of the dispenser, while smiling and saying "Green Team Coronato." He may not understand global warming yet, but he is learning to make more responsible eco-decisions.

Depending on the age of your children, you can all look at ways to solidify that going green is a family event. Host an "Eco-Event" where all members of the family come together to kick off greener living. Activities could include:

- Preparing and serving a green dinner. Try spinach noodles topped with butter and Parmesan cheese. The taste is mild and the consistency is exactly like traditional pasta.

- If after school is an ideal time, gather around the table for sliced green apples with peanut butter or guacamole dip with fresh vegetables or crackers.

- As you're eating, brainstorm ideas for environmental living and write ideas on green construction paper, which can be hung on the refrigerator.

- Come up with a family name or motto to remind you of your commitment to greener living. Our friends, the Close family, came up with the idea of "Getting *Close*r to Nature" and make it a point to spend some time outdoors every day.

- Remember that going green is fun, so avoid using words like "chores" or "errands" at your eco-event. Focusing on activities, field trips, and family time helps set a positive tone for your family.

There are very few "must's" in eco-living. As in, you must drive a hybrid or you must use solar power to heat your home. Instead, enjoy doing the things you discuss at your eco-event. This may even provide an opportunity to broaden the definition of environmental activism. If your kindergartner wants to "help animals," have him go through your linen closet looking for old towels to donate to an animal shelter where they'll be used for bedding. Visiting the shelter provides you all with a chance to donate items that were probably being ignored in your own home, simplifying your household and reusing items in a meaningful way. By having all members of the family share their eco-ideas, you'll have even more opportunities to practice greener living together.

Some of the ideas I suggest will take a while to phase in, while other efforts can be implemented immediately. Instead of replacing all of your appliances with more energy-efficient models, I show you ways to make your current equipment more eco-friendly, and I make suggestions for buying new models when the time is right. Instead of giving up your central heating, I look at ways you can conserve energy while still keeping warm and comfortable. All the while, we'll focus on a team approach that enlists the help of all members of the family. Ages and stages will dictate how everyone participates, but there will always be opportunities for everyone to contribute. And don't worry about being "green enough"; there are no authoritative labels. The goals for all of us are similar: become less of a strain on the environment by reducing our wants, reuse what we already have, and recycle what we can no longer use. We want to build on the good green choices your family is already making. This book can help make your whole family more eco-conscious and help take your efforts even further.

You can approach a greener lifestyle in dozens of ways, and I'll help you find the routine that makes the most sense for your family. With a little preplanning and minimal organization steps, your children can learn to pack lunch for a day at the park; be in charge of bringing along the reusable shopping bags; and make reducing, reusing, and recycling a natural part of their day. Once you get started, you'll notice a slew of personal benefits to going green. Instead of overpaying for fast food, wasting gas money, or over-spending on impulse purchases, you'll find a more environmentally conscientious approach to daily living to save you time, money, and energy—things we all wish we had more of.

Green Groundwork

Building an eco-friendly family takes a strong foundation and a clear direction. We have to know where we are and where we want to go. This helps us to go from making good green choices to embracing great green choices. And since we want to make changes that we can live with on a daily basis, the emphasis will always be on little steps that add up to meaningful miles. Here's an idea of the kind of greater greener-living examples we'll be exploring in depth throughout the upcoming chapters.

1. **Good green living**—When heading into town to run errands, you remember to bring your own recyclable bags.

Great green living—Your children take turns as "Shopper Supervisors," making sure reusable bags are brought from home. In addition to bringing bags, you park in a central location and together walk to several locations while talking about the importance of saving gas. Since you're more likely to be out for an extended amount of time, have children pack a healthy snack to enjoy along the way.

2. **Good green living**—When shopping for beauty products with your tweens and teens, you read the package and look for "no animal testing."

    Great green living—In addition to "no animal testing" you practice "precycling," patronizing manufacturers that use recycled and minimal packaging, or offer customer rewards for returning empty make-up containers.

3. **Good green living**—When packing school lunches, you include a wholesome organic snack like unsweetened applesauce or a granola bar.

    Great green living—In addition to including healthy snacks, you also enlist the help of your children by buying in bulk and then breaking down groceries into reusable single-serving containers. At the store, children can treasure hunt for the best bulk buys, usually located along the bottom and top shelves. Big-name manufacturers who capitalize on selling more expensive single serve purchases pay a premium for product placement at eye level.

4. **Good green living**—When cleaning the house, you use rags instead of paper towels.

    Great green living—In addition to using rags, you all reach for homemade spray bottles, filled with nontoxic ingredients. Since there are no harsh chemicals in your solutions, everyone can help take care of his or her own personal space.

5. **Good green living**—When planning a family vacation, you include a day of outdoor adventure on your itinerary.

    Great green living—In addition to spending time outdoors, you bring along journals and opt to make souvenirs using found treasures instead of buying plastic trinkets. Children can grow with their journals, tracing their hand on the page to mark the date and location of their trip; a personalized reminder of their age and interests.

As you can see, we'll be building on what you already do with suggestions that are meaningful. This is not a race to the finish line, but rather, a marathon based on sustainability. And like any good marathon, we'll take time to stop and rejuvenate ourselves along the way. Throughout the book, you'll find fast "Five-Minute Makeovers" to help keep you motivated and on track. If you're anything like me, a healthy dose of instant eco-gratification can be just the thing to keep you feeling focused. Here's one to get you started.

Five-Minute Makeover

Practice positive, specific, simple language for getting green as a team. For example, instead of saying "We have to eat organic food," have each member of your family choose one new food item to try at dinner. Implement a "two bites without a fight" rule to encourage everyone to try the featured item. Instead of saying "I have to trade in my car for a hybrid," try arranging car pools with other parents to cut down on driving time. Have your computer-savvy kids make up a flyer (on recycled paper, of course!) with your family's contact information. At the next sport's practice, your kids can pass flyers out to their teammates and help find other parents who are interested in sharing driving responsibilities.

Instead of trying to be the one who always comes up with new ideas for going green, give your kids a chance to share their thoughts. Have each member of the family complete the following two sentences and hand their going-green suggestions in a prominent place.

(Proactive) Today I want to (specific)_____

We can all help do this by_____

(Proactive) This week, I want to (specific)_____

We can all help do this by_____

(Proactive) This month, I want to (specific)_____

We can all help do this by_____

Greening Your Family

There's no denying that, as parents, we set the tone for the household and must lead by example. It will most likely be up to us to get the eco-ball rolling at home—but our going-green goal is not all about one parent shouldering the bulk of responsibility while everyone else flies below the radar. It's about each family member doing his oe her share for the collective green good of the home. Chances are, your kids will embrace the chance to make their lifestyle more eco-friendly. Environmental education has secured a place in most schools, with many districts implementing recycling programs, offering fresh options in the cafeteria, and adding environmental studies to the curriculum. Outside the classroom, taking an active role in environmentalism, conservation, and activism has become almost "trendy." Everyone from Hollywood royalty to fashion magazine writers are covering the latest and greatest ways to create a more sustainable future. But unlike style crazes or must-have accessories, environmentalism doesn't have an expiration date. We can no longer turn a blind eye or a deaf ear to the benefits of going green. And why would we want to? Cleaner living is good for us, our families, and our communities. While you may not hear about any actor holding a press conference to encourage taking out the garbage, you're sure to find several photographed in their hybrid cars on the way to a green charity event.

You may be wondering why it is so important to involve our kids in these green efforts. After all, if they are learning about the environment at school and see us recycling, isn't that enough? As much good as I am doing for my family as an environmental enthusiast, there is no denying that I have had to backpedal. I have many bad habits that are hard to break. Almost instinctually, I turn to the waste basket to throw out used computer paper, reach for the individually wrapped serving size, and want to leave on a light before leaving the house. Learning a new way of living, as an adult, means unlearning my old ways.

When we start our children off on the right environmental foot, we begin with good habits that they can build on. In my two-year-old's short life, he has always seen the recycling bins go out with the garbage cans. After the pickup, he drags the recycling container back down the driveway and helps put it back in the pantry closet. He doesn't know any other way. And that's great! I hope that by the time he's an adult, there will be additional means of recycling and any new practices will be an extension of what he already knows. Instead of backpedaling to correct bad habits, he'll be building on his good habits.

Another important reason for teaching our children to make environmentally savvy choices is to help grow the next generation of environmental activists. Our environmental problems cannot just be temporarily addressed and then put on the back burner again. The changes we are making are only beginning to scratch the surface of what needs to be done. By raising our children with a strong sense of respect and reverence for Earth, we help ensure that there will be adults to step into ecological leadership positions.

When thinking about increasing our families' responsibility to sustainable living, it can be reassuring to remember that children are naturally drawn to animals, water, open fields, and trees. While adults are more apt to go "power-walking" down a trail, children enjoy meandering in hopes of finding natural treasures, like rocks, bugs, and flowers. While I appreciate the changing leaves in autumn, my son selects the leaves that impress him the most and hangs them in his playroom. When it comes to kids and the great outdoors, we have a captured audience. Helping them make the connection between running an eco-friendly household and keeping Earth abundant with natural treasures is a meaningful way to introduce environmental awareness. Consider these kid-friendly connections for the younger set:

> When we turn off the water when brushing our teeth, we leave more water for the trees.
>
> By choosing to eat less meat and more vegetarian meals, there will be more cows at the farm.

As children grow and begin to appreciate how precious our natural resources really are, you can continue to make connections:

> When we use our bikes instead of our car, we reduce toxic omissions into the atmosphere, helping to preserve the ozone layer and stop global warming. This means more opportunities

for snowboarding in winter and more enjoyable summer days at the beach. Our choices have consequences—let's choose responsibly.

Indoor air pollution can be just as dangerous as outdoor air pollution, which is why it's so important that we make our own cleaners. Some of the commercial cleaners contain toxins that are just as dangerous as cigarette smoke. Our extra efforts help keep the air we breathe as clean and healthy as possible.

Helping children and young adults see that their decisions have a direct impact on their individual happiness personalizes sustainable living. When we make going green a family value and a personal conviction, we greatly increase the chances of raising environmentally savvy children.

One of the most proactive ways to become a friend to the environment is to simplify. I'll help you target your areas of indulgence and streamline your consumption. For instance, if you tend to throw out food because it has gone bad, planning your weekly meals and shopping locally from a detailed list can help you efficiently use your refrigerator. If your teenager already has half a dozen pairs of black pants but is convinced she needs a new pair, we'll look at ways to update and rotate wardrobes without falling victim to must-have mentality. Simplifying doesn't mean that you have to deny yourself comforts; it means being comfortable with what you already have.

It's best to think of this book as a manual and treat it accordingly. Dog-ear the pages, highlight tips, and write in the margins. Make it your own. As you make notes and write comments, you'll begin to get a better feel for which environmental efforts best suit your family. You'll find ideas that target families who are just beginning to make green choices, as well as more advanced recommendations for households that are farther down the green path. It's important not to get overwhelmed or discouraged if you start feeling "behind." Even the most environmentally friendly homes had to start somewhere. Enjoy the process, let go of perfection, and embrace the opportunity to make a difference in whichever ways you can.

At the conclusion of each following chapter, you'll find a Chapter Checklist that will help you organize your goals and stay motivated. This book has a lot of great ideas; this checklist will help you decide which suggestions and strategies you want to focus on and provides a space for charting your progress. Keeping track of the important changes you make will definitely inspire you to keep going and remind you of how far you have already come.

It is not necessary, or realistic, to implement every idea in this book overnight. You are willing and want to make changes; by doing so slowly and steadily, you will begin to build a solid green foundation for life—and the life of your family. So I am glad to say, congratulations! Welcome to one of the best decisions you've ever made for yourself and the people you love. Whether you are interested in building better recycling habits, conserving water, or looking for ideas on how to host a neighborhood clothing swap, my book will help your family become—and stay—a better friend to the environment. The light is green; it's time to move forward.

Small Changes, Big Results

"Get cash immediately!"

"Log on and find your soul mate today!"

"Quit your job and be your own boss now!"

Not a day goes by without our being bombarded with such sweeping statements. While the subject matter varies, the media's intention is often the same: to convince consumers that big (often immediate) changes are needed to see results. But as we all learned from our friends the tortoise and the hare, slow and steady is usually the way to win a race. A flash-in-the-pan approach may make a big splash or attract a lot of attention, but without a solid plan and staying power, even the best-intended project inevitably goes by the wayside. I have fallen victim to the immediate gratification machine, only to fall short of the mark, and I suspect you have as well. It wasn't until I changed my approach that I began to make real changes in my life.

On my quest to find a healthy diet that works best for my family, I was introduced to a nutritionist whose philosophy focused on organic, whole foods. She encouraged me to find natural alternatives to the processed foods I was used to eating. Instead of using Sweet & Low, I began using Stevia. Instead of cooking with vegetable oil, I discovered grapeseed oil; instead of white flour, almond flour. After initially stumbling to find complementary options, I found my groove, tapping into my health store's personnel for suggestions, logging on to trustworthy websites, and seeking out likeminded families. I didn't "clean house" and toss out my less desirable products; instead, I took some time to work through the products I had on hand while finding replacements that the whole family enjoyed.

I must confess, carob chips are no match for chocolate chips, veggie hot dogs weren't welcomed with open arms (or mouths), and seaweed soup was just too far out there for all of us. But we have greatly changed our diets for the better, even if we do occasionally indulge in old favorites. Today most of those "alternative" choices have become mainstays.

The same correlation can be made with going green. We don't have to give up electricity, or go out and spend money replacing lightbulbs that are working; but replacing burned-out bulbs with more energy-efficient ones is an eco-friendly alternative that you can initiate in your home. Learning which alternatives are available, making a plan for phasing out less-than-ideal practices, and keeping a watchful eye on ways to better manage our current eco-affairs are all positive steps in creating a more energy-efficient household. Going green isn't about giving up what you enjoy, but rather, enjoying things with more environmental awareness. We don't have to stop giving holiday presents, but exchanging homemade gifts, reusing wrapping paper, or even making our own decorative wrap can become fun family traditions that are rooted in greener living.

After reading those examples, you may be wondering, "How big of a difference can these small changes really make?" After all, it makes sense to believe that an environmental crisis would call for extreme actions. But when we focus on what we can do, keeping our plan rooted in reality, we are much more likely to make an important difference in our environment. Actually doing several small *somethings* is much more beneficial than waiting (or hoping) for a chance to make one big change. It may feel like the eco-advantage of taking a shorter shower in hopes of saving water could result in only a drop in the bucket, but rest assured, those drops add up. In this chapter, we focus on a simple mathematical equation that adds up to greener living, review the three cardinal rules of environmentally friendly living that will help govern all of our eco-decisions, and begin to appreciate the benefits of simplifying our surroundings.

Five-Minute Makeovers

Today choose one of these five strategies and take an action step toward greener living. Set a goal to complete the remaining four activities by the end of the month. Small changes like these can set the stage for big eco-results.

The next time you flush the toilet, take the lid off the tank and watch as the water empties out. When the water level is low, place a brick inside the tank to help decrease the amount of water needed to refill the tank. Less water in the tank means less water being flushed down the drain.

Save 20 gallons of water a day by turning on your dishwasher only when there is a full load. Decrease the number of times you need to run your dishwasher by reusing the same drinking glass throughout the day instead of taking a new one for every drink of water.

Increase your fuel efficiency up to 40 percent by driving the speed limit and avoiding sudden braking or acceleration. Less wear and tear on your car also means less wear and tear on the environment.

Bring your own cloth bags when shopping and reduce pollution. Plastic bags are not biodegradable; when they break down, they pollute water and Earth.

Plug your TV, VCR, DVD, and stereo equipment into a single power cord, and turn it off when not in use, eliminating "standby" energy waste.

When we use natural resources more responsibly, we are making a fundamental decision to honor Earth and our place on it. Taking only what we need instead of always indulging in what we want helps ensure that there are enough resources for everyone. Financially speaking, going green can lessen the strain on your wallet. It is often assumed that environmental changes cost big dollars, a price many families cannot afford to pay, despite their good intentions. But by making small changes, financial "start-up" costs remain manageable and the long-term benefits quickly justify the expenditure. Once systems are in place, greener living can help make your household more functional. Greener living means more conscientious shopping. Taking inventory of what you have on hand, organizing what will stay and what will go, leads to less clutter. When there is a place for everything and everything is in its place, shopping routines become more systematic, making the most of your time and energy—and ultimately saving you money. It may be helpful to put these ideas into a useful equation.

Fundamental + Financial + Functional = Forward

Once we make the fundamental decision to take better care of our households—and, by extension, our planet—we do our bodies and our wallets a favor by choosing high-quality, sustainable products whose intention is to add beauty and purpose to our lives; this combination moves us forward toward greener living.

Consider the following statistics from the Earth Day Network (www.earthday.net) in terms of the 4F formula.

Bask in a Bright Idea

If every household in the U.S. replaced a burned-out bulb with an energy-efficient, ENERGY STAR qualified compact fluorescent bulb, the cumulative effect [would be] enormous. It would prevent greenhouse gas emissions equivalent to that from nearly 800,000 cars. It would also save enough energy to light 2.5 million homes for a year.

Fundamental Decision—Responsibly use resources to reduce greenhouse emissions and save energy. When we think of global warming and greenhouse emissions, we usually think cars, power plants, or other large-scale offenders. But making a small-scale change can raise a fixture's efficiency by up to 30 percent.

Financial Benefit—Energy Star models reduce your electric bill about $30 over the life of the compact fluorescent bulb. With an average home having anywhere from 50 to 100 lightbulbs, the more bulbs you replace, the greater the savings. Having an extra $30 to put toward a night out may not seem like a lot, but having an extra $1,500 to put toward a family vacation is worth noting.

Functional Advantage—The right lightbulb will last 6 to 10 times longer than a standard one, meaning less time spent in the dark and less energy spent running to the store. Look for sales on energy-efficient lightbulbs, and stock up so that when you need a new bulb, you have a green alternative ready and waiting.

Forward Living—Bask in the warm light of your smart bulb decisions, knowing that you are using less energy and saving money. Now that you know the benefits of energy-efficient lighting, keep a few extra lightbulbs on hand for a green housewarming gift or a hostess present. Next time a bulb burns out in your friend's house, they will have an eco-friendly replacement at their fingertips. Passing along your eco-awareness helps keep everyone moving in a greener direction.

Stick to a Program

About 42 percent of an average household's energy costs go toward just two things: heating and cooling. Buy a programmable thermostat, which can regulate different temperatures at different times of the day. And if you have one, use it! These thermostats reduce energy use by 5 to 30 percent and save you $100 to $150 in energy costs each year.

Fundamental Decision—Use resources responsibly, to save energy. In the cold of winter and the heat of summer, we are drawn to the thermostat, often adjusting the numbers for optimum comfort. But every time we turn up the heat or cool down the house, we are using precious resources. By making ourselves more responsible, either by putting on a sweater when we want to be warmer or closing the blinds to keep out the sun when we want to be cooler, we can be comfortable inside, no matter what the weather is like outside.

Financial Benefit—When you are sleeping or out for the day, it isn't necessary to heat or cool your house in the same manner as when you are home and awake. In the winter, layer blankets on your bed and turn the thermostat back 10 degrees for 10 hours. This could save 5 to 10 percent a year on heating prices; that's about a 1 percent savings for every degree. In the summer, set the thermostat to cool only when you are home and awake, and enjoy further financial gains.

Functional Advantage—Digital thermostats give you the most program options, meaning you can set your heating/cooling cycles to turn off and on throughout the day and night. Consider the sleeping and working patterns of your household, and set the times accordingly. Once your new system is in place, it requires little maintenance. If you need to make an unscheduled adjustment, most models offer override buttons that do not require resetting the whole system.

Forward Living—If family members have a hard time adjusting to the new temperatures, check to make sure your thermostat is in a good location before demanding more energy from it. Drafts, open doors, bright skylights, and direct sunlight can prevent efficient readings. Set up your family for success, and chances are, your household will cool and heat smoothly.

New and improved lightbulbs and thermostat monitoring are ideas that every family can get behind. Again, we are looking not to completely change our lifestyles, but to make adjustments within our homes to benefit the environment and improve our health. Without having to make drastic changes, we can still make an important difference. With an eco-friendly plan as simple as the 4F equation, it's easy to see that small green-living changes really add up to big eco-results!

Make It Fair Trade

Until recently, I had never really considered where coffee and chocolate, two of my favorite products, came from. I shopped based on sales, looked for generic brands whenever possible, and was happy to try a new product when I found a coupon for it. The more money I saved, the happier I was. Since we drink coffee every day and tend to use chocolate in everything from hot cocoa to baking, I looked for ways to save on both of these pantry staples.

I have come to learn that all these bargains came at a price. Free-trade markets operate on profit. In order for big companies to make the most money, they often seek out factories overseas where labor laws are loose to nonexistent. This means forced child labor, unfair wages, and unhealthy working conditions. You can help change these circumstances by choosing to buy Fair Trade products—like coffee and chocolate.

Our personal consumer choices affect people all over the world. According to *CBS News*, coffee is the world's most important commodity after petroleum. With over 50 percent of Americans drinking three to four cups each day, it's probably safe to assume that the majority of people reading this book are coffee drinkers. This means a significant green difference can be made just by drinking a more socially conscious cup of coffee.

Coffee bushes thrive in shaded areas, and until about 25 years ago, you had to look under a canopy of trees to find coffee shrubs. But in a quest to build a bigger, better bean, agribusinesses developed ways to grow coffee shrubs in direct sunlight using pesticides and fertilizers. Competition for coffee has increased, with smaller, shade-growing farmers finding themselves at the mercy (or lack of) of big business. Major coffee manufacturers can afford to clear fields and grow coffee bushes in direct sunlight using artificial means like pesticides and synthetic fertilizers. Corporate coffee manufacturers clearing trees for coffee fields, contaminating the land with pollutants, and disrupting the natural habitats of birds are just a few of the consequences of cheaper coffee. Smaller, traditional farmers cannot keep up with the competition's production or lower retail prices, making it increasingly difficult for them to make a living. But you can make a difference; environmentally friendly choices are available.

By choosing to buy Fair Trade coffee, you are sending a clear message to coffee conglomerates. Your sustainable purchase helps farmers grow coffee the way nature intended, protects the environment, and supports local economy. According to Global Exchange, the leading online distributor of certified Fair Trade products, the Fair Trade certification signifies that rigorous standards in planting, farming, and labor have been met. Farmers are insured a fair market value for their product, making it possible to grow coffee under optimal conditions and provide workers with a fair wage. Fair Trade products are clearly labeled on the container by a certified third-party organization like TransFair USA, a group that works to promote community growth, health, education, and environmental responsibility. While your kids may not be coffee drinkers, I am hard pressed to find a child who is not a chocolate eater! My husband is completely on board with our family's green lifestyle, with one of his favorite personal contributions being Sunday dinner. Instead of going out to eat on the weekends to give me a break from cooking, my husband suggested that he prepare dinner with the kids on Sunday to save money and energy (and my sanity). Sooner than later, dinner preparations included dessert, and around here that means chocolate. Tom and the boys have mastered the art of homemade peppermint cocoa using Fair Trade chocolate and share their socially responsible treat here:

Ingredients: one Fair Trade chocolate bar, four cups of desired milk (dairy or soy), two candy canes

Parent's job—Pour milk into small pot and heat on low, stirring frequently to avoid scorching. While milk is warming, break chocolate into small pieces and heat on low in a small pot or double boiler, stirring constantly. Do not let scorch. Once melted, remove pot from direct heat.

Kid's job—While Dad is heating the milk and chocolate, the children are preparing the peppermint. Unwrap candy canes and break into small pieces. Place pieces in between layers of wax paper and smash with hammer or rolling pin (this is loud and fun!) Evenly distribute tiny peppermint pieces in four separate mugs.

Once peppermint is in place, pour hot chocolate into each mug, and then add milk. Stir ingredients and sip a sweet Fair Trade treat.

Visit your neighborhood health store to purchase Fair Trade coffee and chocolate. If these items are not available, request that they carry them. If this isn't possible, visit the online store at www.globalexchange.com for a wide selection of Free Trade products, including sugar, honey, snack bars, and nuts. Now that you know how important your beverage and dessert choices are, pass along your knowledge in an attractive manner. The next time you are invited to visit friends, bring along a new bag of coffee or homemade chocolate beverage and share your eco-spirit while sharing dessert.

Family Ties and Tries

The most wonderful thing about making small changes is that even the smallest members of your family can help make a big difference and have fun doing it. The suggestions throughout the book get kids to take an active role in creating and monitoring household changes, making it much more likely that they will take an active interest in the environment. Instead of adding another dull chore to their list, you are helping them participate in your green plans with fun family activities.

For example, if you want your children to be more conscious of using light energy and learn the benefits of energy-efficient bulbs, try keeping a recyclable water cooler container in a high-traffic area like the kitchen. Instead of merely lecturing children to turn off the lights, show them that energy efficiency really pays off. Pull out your last electric bill, explaining that electricity costs money—the same money that is used for trips, clothes, and presents. Challenge your children to save electricity, and money, by turning off lights when they leave a room. Next month, compare your new electric bill with your previous copy and invite members of your helpful household to fill the recyclable container with the pennies you saved. Use your "found funds" on a family outing to help drive home the benefits of environmentally friendly living. Later, expand your conscientious living to include heating and cooling power, television time, and other electronic devices.

If older children are complaining that they are too cold, drop by a consignment store for cozy "new" blankets to add to the TV room. If they are too hot, put them in charge of pulling the blinds on east- and west-facing windows, as this daylight produces unwanted heat and glare. In all instances, help your children find alternatives to reaching for the power and help them empower themselves to make eco-conscious decisions.

Greening Your Teen

There are few things that can deflate a parent's sense of enthusiasm more than a perfectly timed eye roll from their teenager. Since most teens see any change in their routine as a drastic (and dramatic) invasion of privacy, you may suspect that talking to your high schooler about new eco-activities for the family will fall on deaf ears, tempting you to leave them out of any conservation projects. But before frustration leads to isolation, try referencing your 4F equation and encouraging them to be a part of the solution, which may be a more constructive way to address their complaints. I've spoken with some teens, and it seems that one of the biggest motivators for reaching them is money. Now, I am not advocating that we pay our teens to pay attention to the environment, but since you are their primary source of financial assistance, you can draw on this fact.

Instead of the basic equation Fundamental + Financial + Functional = Forward, try moving the elements to better target your teen audience: Forward + Fundamental + Functional = Financial. Let's say you want your teens to stop touching the thermostat every time they feel warm. Instead of making the focus of the conversation the benefit to the environment, make the focus how they can benefit financially. Here's an example:

> Look, I know you feel hot, but using more air conditioning is not our only choice. Why don't you sleep downstairs in the living room tonight, where the ceiling fan will help keep you cooler? And there's a pitcher of ice cold water in the fridge, which can help make you more comfortable. Air conditioning is expensive, so we want to cut back on our costs there; we would rather use the money to send you to snowboarding camp/buy clothes/help pay your car insurance. Let's try having you sleep downstairs and see if that helps.

Chances are, you were going to pay for camp, clothes, and cars anyway. But how you budget the family finances can be a useful way to persuade your teens to get on board with your eco-ideas. Would it be better if your young adults embrace eco-awareness the way you are? Of course. But it might not be realistic. Coming at your teens with ideas and motivations that benefit them, as well as the environment, might be an easier way (for all of you) to get the green balls rolling.

If your teen is finding it especially difficult to take your green advice, try changing messengers instead of the message. Green living is no longer an underground movement, but a front-page story. Websites, movies, and books are media that have joined the Earth-friendly movement and make it easier for you to find the support you need. If your ideas are being met with reluctance, enlist the help of pop-culture resources in an effort to get your teen to rethink environmentalism.

Educational information conveyed in an entertaining way often makes for a much more receptive audience. Host a family movie night that is sure to stir some globally heated discussions by watching *An Inconvenient Truth*. This movie could be dubbed "The Little PowerPoint Presentation That Could": Al Gore's personal conviction to call attention to the global warming crisis inspired him to create the slide show that morphed into an Academy Award–winning movie. During the film, turn off all the lights and focus your energy and energies on this important project (it's available at www.amazon.com).

If your teen loves the Internet, direct her to www.treehugger. com. This site has everything from discussion forums to video contests with smartly written articles. It's the perfect combination of CNN seriousness and Comedy Central spunk. The TreeHuggerTV link offers various short, useful looks at all things good and green. When she is done surfing the site, make sure the computer is powered down and unplugged, saving on standby energy. This site will fast become a bookmarked favorite.

Sirius Satellite Radio has devoted a whole channel to living a more balanced lifestyle. You and your teen might like to check out LIME radio on Channel 114 and tune in to this community of eco-minded talk shows whose spirited discussions and contemporary interviews make getting an earful entertaining. Sirius Radio can also be heard online. For more details, check out www.sirius.com/siriusinternetradio.

The younger set will most likely have an easier time following your lead, but that doesn't mean you shouldn't keep a few of the teen tricks up your sleeve. A new movie, a new website, a new radio station: all small changes that can motivate big changes in attitude and action. Customizing your eco-activities to keep them age appropriate makes it more likely that all members of your household will implement your ideas.

The Cardinal Rules of Green Living

The 3R's of waste management are reduce, reuse, and recycle, and they are, for my family, the cardinal rules of green living. You've already seen some ways that a positive impact in your household is possible by changing the way we shop for, use, and discard products. You may already practice this eco-trinity with weekly recycling pick-ups, product packaging, awareness, and hand-me-downs, or you may be happy to hear that you can start making small changes that make an important difference right now. Whether you are starting at square one or are ready to take your efforts to the next level, you can build on the 3R's and make huge environmental strides with simple, consistent practices.

In the following chapters, we take a look at ideas, strategies, crafts, and recipes for making the most of your 3R lifestyle. But first, let's get into a greener frame of mind with motivating, family-friendly examples that are simple and satisfying.

Reduce

Small Change: Turning off the lights

Big Result: Less energy waste

One of the easiest ways to reduce our impact on the environment is to be mindful of what we are using—and not using. Turning off the lights when we leave the room is often easier said than done. You can purchase and install light sensors on all of your lamps so electricity is turned on when people enter the room and is automatically shut off when they leave. If you would rather make family members responsible for flipping the switch, enlist the help of a "light supervisor" who intermittently walks through the house switching off any lamps or lights that aren't necessary. The supervisor can fine energy wasters and collect penalty pennies for misuse of power. Reduction doesn't mean elimination. Using resources wisely makes for important energy savings. After a predetermined amount of time, ask the "light supervisor" what eco-friendly purchase they would like to make with the collected pennies. Purchasing energy-efficient lightbulbs would be a bright idea!

Reuse

Small Change: Reusing dinnerware

Big Result: Less garbage waste

In a perfect world, everyone in your family would finish up their after-school activities and work obligations in time to wash up and join you at the dinner table for a homemade meal enjoyed on dishware that can be washed and reused. But our busy lifestyles make that idea a novelty more than a norm. Try to limit takeout by planning a weekly menu that includes enough leftovers to store in reusable containers for when you need a quick meal on the run. When you must order takeout, limit waste by assigning a "Picnic Patrolman" to stock and store a "dining kit" in your car, complete with silverware and cloth napkins. This way, you can politely decline plastic ware and paper napkins. When bringing home to-go meals, skip the paper products and condiments, and use your household supplies. Reusing the same product in a new place is another way to expand your 3R practices.

Recycle

Small Change: Recycling paper

Big Result: Less wasted paper

Some days it seems my desk is being taken over by a paper monster. It's very tempting to just start tossing paper in the name of order and using only wipe boards for calendars and lists. While this is a useful practice in many ways, sooner or later you're going to need to write something on paper. Assign a child the position of "scrap saver" and encourage him to leave no sheet of paper unturned. From printer paper to grocery lists, the scrap saver can cut the used sheets in two, flip them over, and store them in conveniently located paper trays for their next use. Recycling doesn't have to take place only outside your home.

Whenever we practice the 3R rules of reduce, reuse, and recycle, we protect natural resources (fundamental step), save money (financial step), and make better use of our time and energy (functional step). Limiting our impact on the environment by minimizing the energy we need is the foundation for eco-friendly living. For those practicing a lifestyle rooted in the 3R's, less becomes more.

Embracing Simplicity

As you begin to really look at your lifestyle through the eyes of an everyday environmentalist, you will see more opportunities to make meaningful changes. A common thread that you will find running through lifestyle changes is the need for less. The higher-quality food you eat, the less food you will need to feel satisfied. The more acclimated you become to respecting the changes of season and dressing appropriately, the less heating and cooling you will use. Taking good care of your appliances, cars, and electronics means you'll need to replace them less often. The realization that we can live happily with less "stuff" marks a shift in our belief system and becomes the driving idea behind our environmental practices.

The "less is more" mantra is beneficial to our purse and the earth. But the more cluttered our homes are, the more difficult it is to accomplish this. The most common culprits keeping us from a clutter-free lifestyle are our closets. The idea of going through your closets may feel like an overwhelming activity; which is why we are not going to tackle all of your home's closets. Just one. Standing in front of your linen closet, ask yourself the following questions:

1. Is everything in this area beautiful and/or useful?
2. How many items here haven't been used for over a year?
3. Do I have multiple items that could be streamlined?
4. Am I hiding items in this closet that are broken and need my attention?
5. Do all of these items help me? Do any of these items hurt my household?

Consider your answers. There's probably room for making improvements in your closet. Try taking 15 minutes and greening your closet with a few simple steps. You could remove stained linens and cut them into rags; gather multiple items and prepare them for donation; glue, sew, or otherwise fix broken items; or refold shelf contents so the items are neat, tidy, and accessible. Whatever is lurking in your closet, address it and simplify the space.

Once you have tackled one 15-minute closet, enlist the help of your children to conquer other closets. Set the timer and tackle the front hall closet, matching gloves that have gone astray, organizing outgrown shoes for donation, and removing any unnecessary papers, books, or toys that have been hidden in the back. The more cluttered our homes are, the less efficiently we can accomplish anything and the more likely we are to buy more of what we already have. When we can't find our gloves, cleats, or library books, we end up getting others. If we have a place for everything and keep everything in its place, we are less likely to buy unnecessary replacements or make isolated, last-minute trips to the store because we just can't find what we need; both of which use up precious resources.

The simple act of spending 15 minutes cleaning out a closet taps into the bigger picture of consumerism. Many times, the "more" factor leads us to live in clutter. We buy another pair of black pants even though we have four pairs, or we end up finding the scotch tape after we purchase a new role. Simplifying our living spaces happens naturally as we practice the 4F equation and come to adopt the 3R's of household management. Living simply doesn't mean we go without, but rather, that we appreciate what we have instead of focusing on what we don't have. Instead of just discarding products or wasting energy, we will be more apt to extend the life of our belongings because they are important to us. By taking care of what we already own, we can become a better friend to the environment. By taking care of one closet at a time, we give ourselves boundaries to work within and a means by which we can measure success. How's that for a simple eco-step?

By looking at your household as a purposeful living space, you are more likely to keep only what you need and only want what you have. That's a wonderful way to reduce your impact on the environment while enjoying your place within it. You don't need to spend an hour on this project; just a few focused minutes will help streamline your closet and lead to more simplified living.

From fundamental decisions, financial benefits, and functional advantages that lead to forward thinking; to practicing reducing, reusing, and recycling; to embracing simplicity—all roads lead to the same destination: a greener household with a strong, green focus, founded on small changes that have big eco-friendly results.

Chapter Checklist

☐ We will focus on small, realistic changes instead of big, complicated ideals.

☐ We will try one of the five-minute makeovers today.

☐ We will think in terms of the 4F equation to move our green goals forward.

☐ We will continue reducing, reusing, and recycling, and build on the systems we have in place.

☐ We will focus more on what we already have and less on what new things we want.

Green Goal Setting

Now that you are ready to move toward greener living, you may be tempted to devote a weekend to completely ridding your house of any and all toxins, setting up recycling stations on every floor, and assigning each family member a list of environmentally exciting projects. While I applaud your enthusiasm, I caution against this approach. An all-or-nothing attitude can quickly lose momentum, causing the projects to derail. At the very least, you'll probably end up turning off the people you are most trying to motivate—the rest of your family. Instead of adopting a strict drill sergeant approach that is more frightening than friendly, we want to attract our family members to embark on this green journey with us. We want the changes we make to last, so we'll need to map out a plan that makes the best use of our efforts and energy. For our purposes, we'll start by looking at a yearlong calendar outline.

At first glance, a year may look like a long time, but taking time to target seasonal eco-friendly choices helps break down our big-picture plan into manageable pieces. Each month lends itself to particular projects, and we want to take advantage of those opportunities. As you read through the rest of the book, you'll find a slew of activities, suggestions, and tips for greening your family. Those ideas can be done in conjunction with the following calendar outline or alone. As the reader of this book, you can decide where to start. You may want to jump in where you are, prepare for the coming month, or wait until your "ideal" season is approaching. Remember, you know your family best. Start slowly, have patience, and choose the suggestions that work best for you.

Working within the natural framework of the season, each month is designed with an eco-topic in mind. The ideas are activity driven, with directions and recipes at your fingertips so you know what to expect as you begin. Since there are four full weeks in every month, I've offered four activities. But don't feel pressured to complete all the suggested activities. If a packed school agenda and out-of-town business make the idea of completing four additional projects seem overwhelming, make that month a time to focus on a single effort. When and how you complete the activities isn't as important as taking action. Even if you try only one new suggestion a month, take pride in your eco-efforts and know that you are contributing to a greener environment.

Peppered throughout the chapter, you'll also find Five-Minute Makeovers, the kinds of quick projects for quick results you first saw in Chapter 1 as you're accomplishing your monthly missions. The ideas in this chapter are easy to implement and need minimal maintenance, helping to make this a calendar of ideas you can build on. I suggest reading through the entire chapter to get a feel for its intention, and making notes where appropriate. For instance, in September we focus on heading back to school, but some states and districts begin the year in August. If this is the case where you live, you may want to consider swapping August and September's itineraries.

This isn't to say that going green is without its bumps in the road. I touch on common setbacks and offer solid logic and inspirational reasoning for moving forward. If your children (read: teens) are especially reluctant to get on board, you may find inspiration at the end of the chapter. I asked reluctant teen environmentalists what would motivate them into action, and I've shared their ideas in a Top Ten Green Teen Activity List. These tough customers may need a bit more coaxing (read: bribes), but this is a case in which the ends truly justify the means.

Once you have decided when to begin, use a wipe-board calendar mounted in a conspicuous location—like the refrigerator—to write one activity on each Sunday to remind everyone of that week's focus. The board can be personalized with additional points of eco-interest like the assignment of a family member to "Eco-Captain," keeping track of recycling days or highlighting an "errands" day to consolidate single visits to the store. With your newly appointed focal point in place, enjoy working together as a family to meet your daily, weekly, and monthly green goals!

January

With colder weather driving families inside, the beginning of the year is a great time to pay attention to indoor energy conservation. Having just spent the holiday season admiring decorative lights, hosting parties, and visiting family, January is an opportune time to recoup from the hustle and bustle. After an extended period of "go, go, go," it is healthy—both physically and spiritually—to take it easy and quiet down your household. But shifting gears from celebrations to solitude isn't always a snap. Since the holidays are so entertaining, family members may find it difficult to enjoy a quiet evening at home. Relying solely on television, computers, iPods, and video games demands a great deal of energy. Finding "old-fashioned" alternatives can offer low-energy, enjoyable options that are fun and eco-friendly.

January is a time for resolutions. If you are starting this book with the intention of going green this year, the following ideas are a nice way to ease into eco-changes. But resolution making is not limited to the first of the year. No matter what month you choose to begin with, make a commitment to stick with your new program. There may be some moaning and groaning in the beginning, as change always brings with it some growing pains. But since the ideas in this book are geared toward fun and function and don't read like "chores," it won't be long before your family begins to see and enjoy the effects of their eco-efforts, both within the household and toward the environment. If you use the monthly plan as a jumping-off point and tweak the suggestions to best fit your own household, family members will look forward to seeing what new green activities are on the calendar—and maybe even add a few of their own.

The Eco-Friendly Four

This month, embrace the New Year with a greener attitude. Make a commitment to try activities and alternatives that bring your family closer together—with each other and with Earth.

1. Host a household "Night In." Choose a low-key weeknight, serve snacks, and invite family members to rediscover the simple pleasure in playing games. Turn off cell phones, computers, and electronics; use only necessary lighting; and get out playing cards or board games.

If you have teens, start in early evening, promising them that you'll play only until a certain time, when they'll be free to e-mail again. If you have younger children, invite them to "freshen up" your game-night materials with these eco-friendly tips:

Clean playing cards by placing them in a used brown paper bag. Add 1 tablespoon of baby powder. Shake the bag vigorously. Remove cards and wipe down with damp rag. Voilà! A fresh set.

Check to make sure all board-game pieces are intact. If you are missing items, keep beans, dry pasta pieces, or wine corks on hand as fill-ins. At the end of the night, use a recyclable plastic container with a lid to store the game pieces so you are organized and ready for the next time.

2. Save energy by making homemade door socks to stop drafts in their tracks. Cut the legs off an old pair of tights, fill with rice or beans, and tie off at the end. For further fun, invite creative little hands to embellish socks with googly eyes; make ears from leftover felt, and add a ribbon scrap mouth to animate your creation into a dog, snake, or other favorite animal. Assign a child the role of "draft detective" to make sure that door socks are in place and doors to rooms that are not in use remain closed.

3. Many households opt to use a humidifier during the winter months to ease breathing, but foul-smelling water isn't a comfort to anyone. Instead of replacing a perfectly useful unit, remember to rinse your humidifier with baking soda between uses. Taking care of what we own helps extend the life of our purchases, limiting our need for replacements.

4. If cold weather and indoor living make you long for the great outdoors, invite it in. Houseplants are natural air purifiers, use no energy, and make an especially welcome health asset when homes are locked up tight during winter months. Children will appreciate the opportunity to take care of the living things that are taking care of them. It is suggested that you have one houseplant for every 100 to 150 square feet of living space. These top five choices are said to help remove the pollutants carbon monoxide, trichloroethylene, benzene, and formaldehyde: spider plants, English ivy, mums, peace lily, and bamboo palm.

Five-Minute Makeover

Pull extra blankets out of storage and remake beds with an extra blanket under the covers so they are more likely to be used. Before bed, lower the thermostat to 65°F so everyone can sleep comfortably with their new blankets while using less energy.

February

The shortest month of the year still has plenty to offer when it comes to the environment. The traditional red hearts of Valentine's Day can be a visual reminder to take care of our own heart health. Proactive health is a mainstay of green living. We don't want to just react to sickness; we want to prevent illness and make more responsible choices by eating better, exercising more, and breathing cleaner air.

When it comes to making personal lifestyle changes, it can be hard to know where to start. I'm not talking about another diet or a grandiose exercise plan. Instead, as is the intention throughout the book, we want to focus on adjustments within our routine. By doing our daily chores mindfully, we can begin to see opportunities to complete everyday tasks with an eye toward environmentalism.

The Eco-Friendly Four

This month, minimal prep time is needed to maximize your eco-abilities. Enjoy taking better care of the environment, while taking better care of you.

1. Eating organic is optimal, but this can be especially challenging in the winter months, as smaller local farms close for the season and supermarkets carry less (or more expensive) selections. Eating your fruits and vegetables is as important as ever, but pesticides can sabotage your efforts. Before food hits your table, have children help you clean your greens. Soak produce in a pot of hot water with 3 to 4 tablespoons of baking soda for five minutes. Use a scrub brush to clean away pollutants and rinse in a pot of cool, clean water. If you live in an area where there is snow, use the discarded water to clean rock salt off your hubcaps. Place the opened container of baking soda in the refrigerator to help absorb smells. Change every four to six months.

2. Take care of the indoor plants that are taking care of you by having children show them some TLC. Apply a dollop of hair conditioner to leaves and let kids gently massage to rid plants of dust and residue. Give them a discarded pair of panty hose to rub leaves gently, removing excess conditioner and restoring luster. Your houseplants will look brand-new! If you like drinking club soda but hate how quickly it goes flat, take notice: plants benefit from club soda's minerals, regardless of the carbonation. Next time you go to pour your drink down the drain, share it with a leafy friend instead.

3. Housework is something we all must do if we want our homes to remain neat, tidy, and inviting, but all that bending and stretching has health benefits, too. If you are in an area that is colder and darker during February, it may be a deterrent to going out and exercising—but housework is good indoor exercise, according to www.healthlink.com. A healthy person who weighs 120 to 150 pounds can burn about 100 calories vacuuming for 25 minutes, mopping the floor for 30 minutes, or ironing clothes for 45 minutes. Although this isn't aerobic activity, it is a step in the right direction. While you are doing what you need to do around the house, try these tips to make your day a little greener:

Make your own natural air freshener. Skip the harsh, artificial fragrances and opt for a chemical-free scent throughout your home by adding a cotton ball dipped in essential oil to your vacuum bag.

When mopping your floors, make tea for two! Steep two fragrant cups of peppermint tea and squeeze half a lemon into each. Combine one cup of tea with one cup of distilled vinegar and swish in bucket. Enjoy your tea while the solution cools. Mop your floor clean, knowing that vinegar disinfects, peppermint tea has antibacterial elements and helps remove scratch marks, and lemon freshens the room.

When you have a load of ironing to do, start with this trick I learned from my mother-in-law. Run the iron over a piece of aluminum foil to clean the surface. Then place aluminum foil underneath the ironing board cover and iron as usual. The foil acts as a conductor, making your ironing more energy efficient since you are ironing the top and the bottom at the same time. Instead of having to go back and forth several times to flatten wrinkles, you are ironing both sides at the same time.

4. Enjoy a family baking activity that is heart-healthy and eco-friendly. Children tend to appear underfoot as soon as the word *cake* is mentioned. Take advantage of your rapt audience by making my No-Sugar & Spice Cake, a hit with all ages and much healthier than store-bought mixes that rely heavily on preservatives and sugar.

No-Sugar & Spice Cake

Yield:	Prep time:	Cook time:	Serving size:
6–8 servings	10 minutes	35-40 minutes	one piece

Dry Ingredients
2 cups pecan flour
1 cup soy flour
2 tsp. baking powder
$1/2$ tsp. sea salt
1 tsp. cinnamon
1 tsp. allspice

Wet Ingredients
2 eggs
1 ripe banana
$1/2$ cup applesauce
1 tsp. vanilla extract
$3/4$ cup milk

1. Preheat oven to 350°F.

2. Grease and flour the insides of two discarded coffee cans.

3. Combine wet ingredients. Then stir wet ingredients into dry.
    Divide batter between two greased coffee cans.

4. Bake 35-40 minutes or until inserted knife comes out clean.
    Let sit 10 minutes upright. Loosen cake from can using a knife.
    Turn over onto cooling rack and let cool completely. Remove
    from can and cut cake into wedges. Serve with fresh fruit.
    Enjoy!

March

With the change of season right around the corner, spring cleaning will soon be in the air. Since we'll soon want to head outdoors
and soak up fresh spring air, March is a good time to prep for the
upcoming season and finish up a few indoor projects along the way.
This March, make a pledge to use less Pledge by trying some homemade cleaning solutions. Today's homes are designed to keep out the
elements, but that means they also keep some unwanted elements
in. Often indoor air is more contaminated then outdoor air due to
cooking, painting, and cleaning within limited spaces. Just because
you can't see the problem doesn't mean it's not there. We'll go into
further detail about green cleaning in Chapter 9, but here are a few
ideas to get you started.

The Eco-Friendly Four

Many hands make light housework. Motivate your kids to become
part of the solution by helping them make their own cleaning solutions.

1. The cleaning spray bottles and scouring powder containers are
probably covered with health warnings. If we want our kids to be
more active participants in taking care of their homes, we first need
to make sure that they'll be safe. This most likely means you have to
change your approach to cleaning. Start slowly with one all-purpose
cleaning solution by mixing ¼ cup vinegar, 1 tablespoon baking soda,
and 1 gallon of water. Fill spray bottles with the kid-friendly solution
and help them host a toy wash at the sink. Gradually weed out toxic
store-bought brands while building your personal cleaning inventory.

2. All this indoor play has probably wreaked havoc on your play-room and family room. No doubt there are broken toys, missing pieces, and crayon markings as evidence of fun. Put your playroom and the toys back together with green solutions. Have children treat the walls to a minor touch-up by rubbing out markings with a damp washcloth dipped in baking soda. Disposable wipe containers, yogurt cups, and oatmeal boxes make for great storage. Candy tins are excellent for keeping small or delicate pieces intact. An old over-the-door shoe holder keeps arts and crafts bits and pieces organized and within reach. Knowing what items we have on hand, and taking care of them, means we need to buy less and replace less often. Help your children develop a sense of ownership now over their crayons, and they'll be more likely to have a sense of ownership over big-ticket items down the line.

Five-Minute Makeover

Keep dirt, grime, and germs outside by insisting that everyone take off their shoes before coming in the house. Keep house slippers nearby and change shoes when coming and going.

3. Get set for gardening by giving your tools the once-over. Sharpen shears by cutting through steel wool several times, and lube blades with castor oil and then buff dry. Get a head start on spring blooms by inviting family members to start seedlings. Check with your local florist or go online to find out the anticipated last frost date for your area, and begin this project about two weeks before that.

After a weekend morning breakfast of eggs, rinse and air-dry the shells. Pin-prick two or three holes in the bottom of each shell, reset-ting them in a cardboard container. Have children lightly fill the shells with soil and one or two seeds. Keep the seedlings moist and warm until they're ready to be transported outdoors. When plant-ing, crush the shells so roots can grow freely, but leave them there as nutrients for the soil. The best time to replant seedlings is after the threat of frost. Since this can vary greatly depending on where you live, a quick call to your neighborhood nursery is your best bet.

4. If crayon drawings are ruining your floors, have children remove the stains by rubbing a dollop of toothpaste over the area with a cloth (mismatched cotton socks are great for this purpose). Treat scratches on wood floors with equal parts lemon juice and olive oil. This solution also makes an excellent furniture polish. With the floors looking tidier, take steps to ensure they stay that way. Prevent unnecessary wear and tear by using old carpet remnants or a tired mouse pad to cut pads for the bottom of your chair legs.

April

Growing plants on your windowsills is an easy and fun way to introduce your children to gardening at any time of the year, with the start of spring being an ideal time to enjoy herbs as they thrive in direct sunlight and warmth. Herbs tend to be hardy, increasing your chances of successful growth. The wonderful thing about growing herbs as a family is that everyone can be involved in each step from planting to pruning to drying to using. Herb gardens offer a long list of activities.

The Eco-Friendly Four

If you live in a home without space for a garden, worry about the time commitment and cost of a backyard garden, or travel in the summer months, herb gardening could be a great option for your family.

Five-Minute Makeover

If insects try to take up residence in your windowsill garden, wash foliage with warm, soapy water to kill pests without harming your plants. Let them air-dry.

1. Start your indoor herb garden with the following supplies:

   3 6" pots to start

   Potting mix—Purchase 1 small bag of sand, 1 small bag of peat moss, and 1 small bag of soil; for each pot, you'll want to have a mix of 1/3 sand, 1/3 peat moss, and 1/3 soil.

Small herb plants, like lavender, from your local nursery

Directions:

Plant ¼ inch down in moist mix—do not saturate.

Place pots on sunny windowsills, where herbs will receive direct sunlight four to six hours a day.

Mist plants with a spray bottle every other day to keep herbs moist.

2. Once your herbs start to grow—usually in about two to three weeks—you'll be ready to prune them for drying.

Trim healthy branches off your herb plant, removing low leaves. Tie three to four branches together using kitchen string, or wrap a rubber band around the bottom stem. Punch holes in a reusable brown paper grocery bag and place bundles in bag upside down. Bunches should have plenty of room to "breathe." Hang bag in warm space; ideally, suspend it over the windowsill. In about 10 days, check the herbs. Once they're dried, you're ready to prepare them for storage and use.

3. Properly storing herbs means you'll always have what you need on hand. Dried herbs should be kept in airtight containers. This is a great time to reuse plastic containers! Keep herbs whole and on the branch until you're ready to use them. When needed, pluck leaves and place them between layers of wax paper. Roll a rolling pin or can over the leaves. You can also crush them between your fingers. Store unused, dried herbs in a dark, cool pantry for up to a year, discarding any moldy leaves immediately. As a rule of thumb, 1 teaspoon of dried, crushed herbs is the equivalent of 1 tablespoon of fresh herbs.

4. You can use lavender in a variety of ways to promote relaxation. Its pleasant fragrance is best enjoyed naturally; artificially produced lavender tends to smell sickly sweet and is often overpowering rather than soothing. Try these sachets at home or make several and give away as gifts.

Sweet Dreams Sachets. If your children suffer from restlessness and have a hard time going to or staying asleep, help them make these sachets. Pluck several lavender leaves from a branch, crush, and place in center of small 2×2 square of cheesecloth. Bring the sides together and tie them with ribbon. Place the sachet inside your child's pillow case right before bedtime.

May

Having just spent a season inside, you've probably greatly relied on electronic entertainment. Give your fuse box a much needed rest, and yourself some much needed exercise, by spending more time outside. It can be hard to get motivated off the couch, especially when we're used to associating spring cleanups with additional, unwanted work. But we'll be concentrating on the physical and spiritual benefits of this season by focusing on eco-elements that make the great outdoors, great.

If you are drawn to the outdoors, a camping trip with tips for using recyclable materials could be just the thing to get your family excited about expanding their eco-efforts. If, on the other hand, your favorite terrain requires 18 holes, you can still make more positive environmental choices. This is also a wonderful time of year for reconnecting with your children. The spring season is naturally entertaining and plays host to a wonderful combination of tranquility and exhilaration.

The Eco-Friendly Four

The more time we spend with nature, the more opportunities we have to strengthen our bond with it. Numerous sources have cited how disconnected we are becoming from our natural environment. This month, become an exception to that unhappy trend and forge a greener trail.

1. Get dirty. Playing in mud puddles, collecting rocks, and pulling up dandelions are wonderful sources of entertainment and reacquaint us with Earth. Encourage your kids to bring along a tote bag to carry their Earth treasures. Pack a picnic dinner in recyclable containers and head to the park for a late afternoon filled with unstructured play. Take time to introduce yourself to other families who are enjoying themselves and pass along a kind word. Feeling connected to our environment and our community helps remind us that the positive effects of greener choices branch out beyond ourselves.

2. The sounds of spring can be heard at all the ball fields. Get ready for a new baseball season by softening your baseball lover's glove using olive oil. Have your child rub the glove all over, place a ball in the mitt, and then tie it with twine to make the glove soft and more pliable. As sport teams take to the field, lend your green support with homemade noisemakers. Have the kids fill the cardboard rolls from toilet paper with dry beans, cover them with scrap paper, and then embellish with color.

3. If golf is your game, recycle gently used aluminum foil to polish your club shafts. After playing a round, wipe down the club heads with olive oil and buff dry. Golf shoes can also work wonders on early spring grass. Stuff the toes of adult golf shoes with an extra sock and fit them on junior before you send him running across your lawn. This fun "monster mash" is also eco-functional, helping aerate the lawn so more oxygen and water reaches the roots.

4. As you get packed for a camping trip, reevaluate your tools of the trade by visiting your recycling bucket for inspiration. A discarded coffee can is the perfect place to keep your toilet paper dry, meaning less waste and less mess. An empty toilet tissue or paper towel roll stuffed with recycled newspaper is an excellent source of kindling and can be prepared before setting up camp. When you're ready to start your campfire, reach for your dry matches wrapped in used aluminum foil and reuse those trick birthday candles from your last celebration. They are less likely to blow out and can be used again and again.

June

With the days longer and the weather warmer, this is the ideal month for completing yard projects. Although it is easier to just pay some-one to tackle your yard, tending the grounds around your home is spiritually enriching and physically invigorating. Turning outdoor projects into family activities makes for cost-efficient memories, and you can use the money you save to upgrade your projects. Save on hired labor and splurge on more flower beds, a high-quality walkway, or swing set equipment.

Growing media coverage over the last few years has focused on the risks of sun exposure and the threat from insect bites. This has frightened many families into believing that the outdoors is dangerous. While we can—and should—take precautions, such a sweeping assumption illustrates how disconnected we have become from treating Earth as our home. The outdoors is not "out to get us." This month, take time to enjoy your big backyard.

The Eco-Friendly Four

Instead of always having to head out to pricey theme parks or drive long distances, stick close to home and enjoy creating an outdoor oasis while keeping company with those who mean the most to you.

1. Enjoy the outdoors without being bothered by flies and mosquitoes by creating your own natural insect traps. Combine boiling sugar, corn syrup, and water until a paste forms. When it cools, have your children spread it on a brown paper bag, which you hang nearby. Reuse your winter vapor rub, and help repel ticks and mosquitoes by applying the ointment to legs and pants. If wasps are trying to nest in your yard's birdhouse, hand your kids a bar of regular soap and instruct them to rub it all over, which will deter pests. Pets who enjoy being outside but don't like sharing their food with ants, or pesticides, will appreciate having their dishes placed within a larger bowl of soapy water.

2. Make fast work of erecting a swing set, tending a garden, or laying a brick path by organizing a working playdate and inviting friends and family to help. Supply materials and refreshments, and have some functional fun. For little gardeners with tender knees, make eco-gear using cleaned grocery foam trays (the kind meats are usually packaged with) as knee pads, kept in place by sliding the cut-off top of a mismatched tube sock over it.

3. Instead of paying for expensive, heavily treated flowers from the florist, put together a flower bouquet from your personal garden or visit a community garden and enjoy their selection. You can also have children dry flowers by picking them, tying the stems together, and hanging them upside down in a warm, dry place for four weeks. This

is a great time to stock up on the season's flowers and complete a drying project in anticipation of upcoming birthdays or graduations.

4. As spring changes to summer, be aware of the sun's strength. Insist that kids wear broad-brimmed hats, sunglasses, and loose, light clothing to provide protection from the sun. Everyone should drink plenty of water to remain hydrated and to help skin stay moisturized. Elect one child "Water Watcher" and keep a pitcher of water close by for refills. The sun is strongest during the middle of the day, so garden in the early morning (before insects are active, too) and play in the shade during the afternoon. Opt for natural sunscreens that contain ingredients like shea butter, jojoba oil, zincs, and green tea. And a study from the American Journal of Clinical Nutrition has shown that increasing your vitamin A an additional 25 mg and vitamin E an additional 335 mg can help diminish your body's sensitivity to UV light.

July

With the kids out of school and summer in full swing, July is the perfect time to patronize your area's farmers' market. Buying local produce is a surefire way to support your local economy, enjoy vitamin-dense fruits and vegetables, and avoid overpackaging. Introduce yourself to the family who owns the local farm stand so your children associate a name and face with the farm, helping to personalize the experience.

If you find that your regular routine leads you to the supermarket, where the "since I'm already here, I'll just get what they have" habit is making it hard to head to the farm stand first, organize your shopping list by writing "Farmers' Market" at the top of the list as a visual reminder. Include your youngest children in this new practice by always singing "Old McDonald Had a Farm" when you get in the car to run errands.

The Eco-Friendly Four

When children learn firsthand that Earth, not the supermarket, supplies our food, they can better appreciate their responsibility to take care of it.

1. When picking out fruits and vegetables, talk about what "shopping in season" means. Explain that while the supermarket may carry more of a selection, the price for bringing food so far—gas, excessive packaging, and unnatural demands on Earth—is a strain on the environment. Buy one apple from the farmers' market and one from the supermarket. Compare the skins, sizes, and shapes. Explain that fertilizers and pesticides may make an apple look more appealing, but looks can be deceiving. The closer we are to food's natural state, how and where it is grown, the healthier it is for us.

2. Host a kid-friendly taste test by blindfolding family members and setting out in-season, local fruit and imported, store-bought fruit. Compare the difference and talk about the results. Assign children the role of "Market Master" and encourage them to pick a new treat from the farm stand each time you go. Give the new fruit or vegetable special attention at the table.

3. If insects are threatening your garden, try this kid-safe bug repellant: combine 3 hot peppers, 5 cloves of garlic, 3 tablespoons of eco-friendly liquid soap, and 1 tablespoon of vegetable oil in the blender and pureé. Strain through cheesecloth and fill a spray bottle with the solution. Test-apply to one leaf—some plants react poorly to oil—and note that bug repellants do not discriminate between beneficial and harmful bugs, so have children spray sparingly.

4. Local farms pride themselves on using fewer pesticides and minimal packaging. Fresh herbs are healthy and aromatic, but recipes often call for a small portion of what you have bought. Instead of throwing out the remainders or letting them go bad, add herbs to your next cookout. Have the children pick apart mint leaves, place them in ice trays, fill with water, and freeze for a more flavorful cup of iced tea. Toss sage and rosemary onto your barbeque coals to help repel flies and mosquitoes while you cook. Place the remaining mint

leaves on small dishes or in sachets around picnic dishes to deter flies while you're eating.

August

With a new school year fast approaching, now is the time to expand recycling from the kitchen to other rooms in the house. We're used to recycling our plastic bottles and newspapers in the kitchen, but there's a lot of living—and, unfortunately, wasting—going on throughout the house. There's another place (besides the garbage can) for computer paper and printer ink cartridges, clothing, shoes, cell phones, and video cassettes. The key is to have systems in place so when a family member is holding an unwanted item in his hand thinking "What do I do with this?" there is a receptacle ready and willing to answer the question.

The Eco-Friendly Four

When we implement recycling programs throughout the house, what we are really doing is expanding our view of how we can help the environment. With enough practice and enough opportunities, we will look at all areas of our life through green-colored glasses.

1. Once school starts, so do computer projects. This year, put a dual-can practice into place wherever you have a printer. Mark one can "garbage" and one can "paper only." If your wastebaskets don't have lids, reuse a piece of cardboard from an old box and attach a home-made lid that has to be lifted. This way, no one is absentmindedly dropping paper into the garbage can or vice versa. Before computer paper ever hits the recycling container, make sure you have used both sides. Set up a paper tray for collecting sheets that can be used again. When it's time to purchase a new ream, look for recycled paper products.

2. The next time you head to your local deli or favorite neighborhood restaurant, ask the manager if you can have some of the 5-pound buckets they receive for food deliveries. These buckets, once cleaned, are ideal recycling containers to keep in closets; they're sturdy, they're tall, and they have handles. Put a container in each of your children's closets, and your own, so when a shirt is outgrown

or shoes are retired, they have a place to go. Round up your buckets periodically and donate items to worthy causes. Many charities accept clothes, but it can be harder to find a place for your shoes. Here are a few ideas:

- Soles4Souls accepts gently worn shoes and delivers them to people in need, like Hurricane Katrina victims. Mail your shoes to Soles4Souls Inc., 2900 Lebanon Road, Nashville, TN 37214, or contact them at www.soles4souls.com.

- When you outgrow your Crocs, mail them to 1510 Nelson Road, Longmont, CO 80501, and they'll be shredded to make children's playground padding. Clearly mark the outside of your package "Recycle."

- Nike's Reuse-A-Shoe Program accepts all brands of athletic shoes and grinds them up to use for new sports surfaces, like basketball courts. Check out www.nike.com/nikebiz for a drop-off location near you, or mail any number of shoes to Nike Recycling Center, c/o Reuse-A-Shoe, 26755 SW 95th Avenue, Wilsonville, OR 97070.

3. If you have technological odds and ends—an old computer mouse, cell phones, computer keyboards and wires, rechargeable batteries, and the like—or big-ticket items like old computers and modems, check out www.greendisk.com. For a reasonable shipping and handling price, this company will reuse or recycle all of your "techno-trash." If during this school year you're upgrading your tech support, make a green transition with help from this site.

4. Don't underestimate the savings by recycling within your own house. In addition to the classic "hand me down" approach, always be on the lookout for ways to reuse what you have on hand. Empty baby wipe containers make excellent plastic bag dispensers, summer berry baskets can conveniently hold rolls of twine and make tying up recycled newspapers easier, and stained shower curtains make useful drop cloths for school art projects or can be cut to use as an art apron. Designate a closet or pantry shelf for potential recyclable containers. Before you head out to buy something new, check your environmentally friendly shelf for eco-savings.

September

Back-to-school sales now rival those of the holiday season rush. Advertising moguls insist that students *need* new clothes and new materials for every new school year. While September is a new beginning, we can help our children move away from dissatisfied consumers and toward satisfied environmentalists.

It is highly unlikely that you'll find a kid who doesn't want the latest and greatest trend in everything, especially when all of her friends have it. But taking a good look at materials you already have on hand and then making well-informed decisions about a few choice items to round out your wants is a huge step in the right direction.

The Eco-Friendly Four

Convincing your kids, and yourself, that new isn't necessary isn't always easy at first, but it is easier on your wallet and the environment. With the emphasis on new and fun ideas, you can look at school as another area in which to develop strong green roots.

1. Assign young children the role of "Have on Hand Policeman" and encourage them to patrol your home looking for supplies you already own. Allot points for the most pens, pencils, and crayons found, and award the winner with first choice of the loot. After children scour the house and turn in their findings, give them a place to put leftover scraps of colorful ribbon, inkless pens, coloring book pages, and the like by labeling a recycled box "Treasures." Once it is filled, spend an afternoon creating crafts out of your "new" supplies.

2. For school supplies that need a facelift, enlist the help of your kids to breathe new life into older materials. In our throwaway society, taking the time to take care of what you have is an invaluable lesson.

- Sharpen scissors by cutting through a used piece of aluminum foil folded several times. Lubricate with a good dose of castor oil and wipe clean.
- Buff up leather backpacks and shoes with cotton cloth and baby oil.

- Remix craft paint by dropping two or three marbles in the container and shaking vigorously.

- Sharpen pencils and save shavings in a matchless sock. Then pack the sock with winter sweaters to help prevent moths.

- Unwind a paperclip and use the end to unclog glue bottle tops.

- Soften hard paintbrush bristles by soaking them in vinegar for five minutes, massaging the bristles, and then rinsing.

3. If the summer sun has done a number on your tween's hair and face, and she is clamoring for an expensive trip to the salon, try these all-natural home remedies instead. Having a Back to School Spa party with friends is a fun green way to detoxify hair and skin without toxic chemicals.

- Treat chlorine hair by rinsing it with club soda.

- Whiten teeth by applying a small amount of baking soda to them after a regular brushing. Don't rinse.

- Indulge in a post-summer three-step facial. First, boil water and pour it over two herbal tea bags. While the tea steeps, exfoliate skin by combining sea salt (larger grains than table salt) with olive oil and gently rubbing into skin using a washcloth. Rinse well and pat dry. Remove tea bags from water and let cool. Apply fresh lemon juice, a natural astringent, to a cotton ball and swipe entire face and neck. Lastly, combine ½ cup of oatmeal with ¾ cup milk. Microwave two minutes. Stir in 1 tablespoon of honey. Let mixture cool to a comfortable temperature and apply a thin, even layer to face. Place tea bags over eyes and relax with oatmeal facial for 10 minutes. Rinse well with cool water and pat face dry.

4. Be the change you want to see by streamlining your home office space or kitchen vanity. After cleaning and drying recyclable cans of different sizes and shapes, join them together using a hot glue gun. Fill with pens, pencils, scissors, and tape. Use earrings whose match is missing as decorative "thumbtacks" on your cork board. Protect your hardwood floors by cutting up an old mouse pad into small squares to use on the bottom of chairs.

October

As the days draw shorter and the air grows cooler, it's time to change over the closets' contents. Surrounded by two seasons' worth of clothes (at least) and a multitude of miscellaneous items, October is the perfect time to simplify all that "stuff." Breaking away from the belief that the more we have, the happier we are, and internalizing that the happier we are, the more we have, is really the crux of reduce, reuse, and recycle.

It can be hard to part with things because we think that as soon as we give it away, we'll need it. But in the meantime, we continue to buy more, making it nearly impossible to use or appreciate any of it. A closet makeover based on the standard that all possessions should be beautiful or useful (and, hopefully, both) can be the first step in simplifying our entire household.

Eco-Friendly Four

Cleaning out your closet can result in much needed charitable donations and helps you better use and care for the things you keep. Raising responsible consumers means helping our children organize their belongings with an eye toward everything in its place and a place for everything.

1. With your children's help, wash and fold a load of outgrown clothes your neighbor or a friend would appreciate, and hand-deliver the box. First, try to remove any stains with a simple solution of baking soda, water, and dish liquid mixed in a spray bottle. Replace missing buttons, patch a rip, or unstick a zipper. Treating donations with the same respect you would treat any gift brings a sense of reverence to your recycling activity.

2. Gather up outgrown stuffed animals, games, and puzzles, and have kids give each item a full inspection. Give deflated animals a lift by filling in the stuffing with beans, and sew on new eyes, ears, and the like where necessary. Wipe down puzzles and game pieces with vinegar and water, to disinfect. Neatly repackage game pieces and tape boxes, if necessary. Contact your town library and see if they would accept your donation for their children's room, or call a children's hospital and offer your donations. Project Smile is a nonprofit

organization that collects like-new stuffed animals that firefighters and police officers can distribute to children during a traumatic time. Visit their website (www.projectsmile.com) for guidelines and contact information.

3. Take better care of the things you want to hold on to by organizing your closet space. Use a discarded ice cube tray to hold jewelry or small toys. Keep shoes fresh by filling mismatched socks with baking soda and stuffing them in the toes. Assign everyone a personal coffee can (younger children can decorate theirs) and keep them on a shelf in the laundry room to use when cleaning out pockets. This also helps take better care of your washer and dryer.

Five-Minute Makeover

If you have younger children who will benefit from hand-me-downs, section off their closets to better organize their clothes. Try making "Wear Right Now" and "Wear Late This Season" locations to stay on top of expanding wardrobes. For older children who will not inherit clothes from siblings, section closet space into "Favorites," "Sometimes," and "Never" sections with a wipe board mounted for "Want" to write down desired additions. Before new things are bought for a wardrobe, "Never" items can be donated and "Sometimes" items can be given an accessory update, tailored, or shared with a sibling. Ideally, everything in everyone's closet should have a purpose.

4. Halloween is tailor-made for children, but all that potential candy consumption might be the most frightening thing about this holiday. You don't have to skip out on the fun, but consider saving the bulk of your candy to use during the upcoming holidays. After sorting through the stash, give children a number of treats they can enjoy over the following days. Keep the rest in the freezer until early December, when you can defrost it and use it to decorate a "gingerbread house" cookie using graham crackers; a much easier project to accomplish with younger kids. Look for graham crackers that can easily be broken into four equal pieces. Break the cracker in half and

cover this entire square with icing. Break the remaining square in half, cover with icing, and press onto top of first square on a diagonal to create a roof. Decorate your "gingerbread house" cookie with candy windows, door, and chimney. Cleaning out the freezer and looking for the candy will be one of the easiest tasks you ever assign.

November

In the days or weeks leading up to Thanksgiving, take time to acknowledge loved ones by practicing simple acts of kindness. With everyone's busy schedule, it's easy to forget the important role we play in each other's lives. We skimp on manners and compliments because we're in a rush. Add to our routines the impending holiday chaos, and we find ourselves short on patience, too. This month, make a conscious effort to stop, look, and listen—to be present. Part of raising an environmentally friendly family means having a friendly environment inside our own homes.

This is also the time of year to thank the people who make your life run smoothly but are often taken for granted. Mail deliverers, neighborhood cashiers, sanitation workers, and cafeteria staff all deserve acknowledgement. Often we think about nice things to do for them but fret that our ideas wouldn't be good enough, so we put off any token of appreciation at all. A modest thank-you project that is actually completed is much more appreciated than grandiose good intentions that never get off the ground. A jar of homemade tomato sauce, a container of trail mix or a batch of cookies delivered with a thank-you note is a meaningful and much appreciated gesture of goodwill.

The Eco-Friendly Four

It's never too early, or too late, to benefit from gracious practices. Gratitude for those in our homes and those in our community helps us feel connected and remain right-sized, two critical elements of healthy living.

1. Encourage your kids to show their gratitude for the great outdoors by creating a centerpiece with rocks, leaves, or pinecones in lieu of a store-bought item. Recycle a used aluminum pie pan and affix candles to it by melting the candle on the bottom and pushing

it into place. Arrange natural treasures around the candles. Each evening, light these gratitude candles and take turns thanking the people in your lives—bus drivers, mailmen, store clerks, and so on—who make daily tasks run smoothly.

2. Depending on your household's schedule, choose an evening or morning when everyone will be home, and take turns expressing your appreciation for one another. Using a random, mismatched place setting that was probably headed to the garbage, set the table as usual, setting the "special plate" for someone. During the meal, each person must say one thing they admire or appreciate about this person. At the next mealtime, the plate moves to another guest of honor. While an activity like this may feel a little "out there" at first; remember these words spoken by Lao Tzu, credited with being the father of Taosim:

> If there is to be peace in the world,
> there must be peace in the nations.
>
> If there is to be peace in the nations,
> there must be peace in the cities.
>
> If there is to be peace in the cities,
> there must be peace between neighbors.
>
> If there is to be peace between neighbors,
> there must be peace in the home.
>
> If there is to be peace in the home,
> there must be peace in the heart.
>
> —Lao Tzu (570–490 B.C.E.)

3. When we are too busy to pay attention to our surroundings, we start to lose focus on the "big picture." While it may not seem like a big deal to always be so busy, rushing from one place to the next leaves us little time to actually enjoy our day, let alone think about making more eco-friendly decisions. Do yourself and your family a favor by remembering to "Take Five" the next time you are running errands:

> *Slow down and smile.* Set your watch a few minutes fast and take a moment to exchange pleasantries with the people you are interacting with, confident that you are not running behind.

Dust off your "please" and "thank you" manners, and remember to model good etiquette. Before asking a salesperson for what you want or need, smile. It may be the only smile that person receives all day.

Pack your purse or diaper bag the night before you have a long day out. Bring snacks from home and cloth bags for purchases, and fill water thermoses to avoid having to buy what you already own.

Look at your to-do list and mark your top three chores. After you complete those, reevaluate whether you have to continue down your list. Tired bodies make tired decisions. Choose to quit while you are ahead whenever you can.

Whenever possible, plan your day so you can park in a central location and walk to different locations. Try to take any opportunity you can to get your family into the fresh air; it's invigorating and can naturally refresh your spirits.

4. The holidays are a special time to spoil out-of-town guests and extended family, but don't forget about taking care of the people who live right under your roof. Enjoy some aromatherapy by simmering a soothing stovetop potpourri everyone can enjoy. Some store-bought scented candles and air fresheners are manufactured with chemicals that have been linked to respiratory problems. Avoid this air pollution by sticking to natural products and making a "Seasonal Simmer":

> Slice 1 orange and 1 lemon, and have children stick cloves into the skin. Place in saucepan with 3 cinnamon sticks and 1 bay leaf. Cover ingredients with 2 cups apple cider and 1 cup water. Simmer on low, adding more water or apple cider as needed. If you prefer to use a crock pot, double the recipe and set on low.

December

The season of giving all too often turns into the season of griping. This is a month when we can easily lose focus of our values and get caught up in the "want" machine. Our "Reduce, Reuse, and Recycle" mantra can't be heard over the roar of the mall crowd, and our efforts to simplify seem simple-minded. But before you collapse under the pressure of another commercialized Christmas, consider giving your family the best gift you can: greener living.

I am a huge fan of presents, as both the giver and the receiver, and I have spent many an hour poring over catalogs in hopes of buying the perfect present, preparing the perfect meal, and hosting the perfect holiday. Usually I am exhausted by midmonth. It took me a long time to realize that the holidays are a season, not just a day. I don't have to participate in a race to the cashier's line. I can cut back, calm down, and actually enjoy the season by not detouring too far off my green path. Here are some suggestions to help you enjoy eco-holidays.

Five-Minute Makeover

Instead of berating yourself for all the things you still haven't had a chance to do this year, spend five quiet minutes a day reminding yourself of all the things you have accomplished and all the gifts you already have.

The Eco-Friendly Four

This month provides an excellent opportunity for replacing our old behaviors with new environmentally responsible actions. Take care of yourself, and Earth, with ideas based on values you've been practicing all year long.

1. Instead of buying a gift for everyone in your family, organize a secret Santa exchange with family members to cut back on over-spending. Taking the time to choose one meaningful present that reflects your relationship or celebrates your recipient's interests is much more meaningful than haphazardly buying impersonal trinkets. If age appropriate, have cousins swap toys with each other in lieu of buying new presents.

2. Instead of buying numerous ingredients for several different kinds of desserts, bake batches of the same cookies, pack them in recycled containers, and use them as gifts, along with a personalized

note. Oatmeal containers and coffee cans, decorated by loving hands, are the perfect size for delivering your homemade treats.

3. Instead of trying to squeeze in an expensive night out with your family during a jam-packed season of parties, reconnect with a "night in" complete with seasonal music and holiday cheer. Skip the long lines at the movies and watch a family favorite. Get ready for the holiday by making your own wrapping paper using recycled brown paper bags from the supermarket. Cover paper with handprints or footprints, and use leftover scrapbooking materials, decorative stamps, or original artwork. Skip the expensive and environmentally unfriendly store-bought wrap and go green together.

4. Instead of throwing out all of those shipping boxes and the packaging materials they're filled with, turn them into useful winter projects. Oversized boxes make excellent forts, playhouses, and castles for children home on school snow days, and bubble wrap can be reused to wrap delicate decorations. Styrofoam popcorn packaging is handy for shipping future presents or to use for simple craft making.

Breaking down our green goals month by month over the course of a year is an effective way to work wisely. Your family can build on this calendar in the coming years, keeping the activities that were fun and functional and adding new ideas to better suit your needs. By approaching going green on a daily basis, you'll be taking local steps that have a beneficial global impact.

Green Teens

After speaking with several teens about their environmental views, one thing was clear: two very separate camps reside in the local high school hallways. On one hand are students who are very eco-savvy and who have creative and practical ideas for being more responsible eco-consumers. On the other hand are young adults who, to paraphrase what our babysitter said, are not going to go out of their way to help the environment. The preceding calendar is filled with family-friendly ideas that you can adjust to fit the age and interest level of your children. But if you're finding that your teen is more resistant than you expected and much less enthusiastic than you hoped, here are 10 eco-friendly ideas from teens for teens:

1. Finding ways to keep more of their hard-earned cash in their own pockets is high on every teen's list. Give them the keys to the car, and send them to the gas station on their way home from school or for errands to have the tires checked and air filter changed. Properly inflated tires can save up to 10¢ a gallon, and a clean filter can save up to 32¢ a gallon. This is an eco-activity that directly affects their wallet.

2. After a household closet cleanout, send your outgrown and unwanted things to the consignment store via your teen. For his efforts, he gets to keep the money made on any clothes sold, and you get a more organized home.

3. If your teens love the smell of candles or perfumed plug-ins, but you know the health risks of adding more pollutants to your indoor air, offer a healthy alternative. A dab of vanilla extract on a hot lightbulb can fill a room with fragrance instead of contaminants.

4. Teens eager to redecorate their room can make their own recycled borders by nailing discarded CDs to the wall and framing their room in music.

5. School art projects can be recycled for holiday presents to grandparents. Framing a painting or setting a clay pot in a shadow box is an easy way to opt for personal gift giving instead of buying consumer products.

6. Mailed invitations aren't necessary with online invitations. Save paper, postage, and travel time, and opt for e-vites. Teens are happy to set up the e-vite message and send it out for you.

7. Teens are likely to respond favorably to healthy eating, as it helps them look and feel good. Eating less meat and more vegetables and grains is not just good for their health; it's good for the environment. According to the Environmental Defense website www.enviromentaldefense.org, "If every American had one meat-free meal per week, it would be the same as taking more than five million cars off our roads." Give teens the task of making a nonmeat dinner one night a week, and enjoy lighter fare like salads, cheese, fruit, and sandwiches.

8. Plastic water bottles are eco-nightmares, but teens love the convenience and leak-proof tight cap, a problem with traditional thermos bottles. Celebrate the start of a new sports season with

a Clean Canteen, available at www.amazon.com. These sleek stainless-steel canteens are 100 percent recycled, come with a variety of caps, and always produce clean-tasting water.

9. A picture is still worth a thousand words. Ask your teen to download an eco-inspirational screen saver so that when he's at the computer, he'll always have a gentle green reminder waiting for him.

10. For her birthday, in addition to the present she asks for, make a donation in your teen's name. Ask her to choose the eco-charity she would like you to patronize. This Internet research just might spark a new environmental interest.

You now have an entire year of eco-friendly tips in your hands. The following chapters target specific areas of opportunity on our quest to grow greener households to complement the seasonal overview we have just discussed. Deciding when and where to begin is up to you; enjoy the process and celebrate the results.

Chapter Checklist

☐ We will post the calendar ideas as a reminder of our family's eco-goals.

☐ We will remember that the calendar is a guideline and make adjustments to suit our household.

☐ We will look for opportunities to give our children more green responsibilities.

☐ We will reevaluate our strategies when dealing with resistant family members and try new tactics.

☐ We will break down our long-term goals into manageable short-term projects.

Reduce: Diminish the Damage

When we look at Earth, and our place on it, through the context of supply and demand, we can more easily see why we must make strides in reducing our waste. Earth doesn't have a maximum capacity sign hanging from its shingle, but the truth is, we are beginning to cramp its style. Like the consummate hostess who lets more people into the party and then ends up racing around to divvy up dishes and find more seating, we have taken advantage of Earth's hospitality.

Let's start with a basic truth: there's only one Earth, and it has a limited supply of resources. Even resources that are renewable, like trees, depend on other natural resources to grow. Nothing on our planet lives in isolation. *Everything* is connected. Down the drain, in the garbage, or up in smoke … it all ends up somewhere: our water, our land, or our air. An out-of-sight, out-of-mind approach to the environment won't serve us well. Appreciating that all of our actions have consequences is crucial if we really want to make a positive eco-impact.

In the United States, it is culturally accepted, even revered, to have more, grow bigger, and expand further. We tend to define ourselves through status-symbol possessions and enjoy being the first ones on the block with the latest and greatest in convenience and comfort. By no means am I wagging a judgmental finger, as I, too, appreciate my comforts and look forward to new things. The problem is that we're spending too much time wanting more and not enough time appreciating and using what we already have. Our current cup runneth over, yet we're insisting that the overworked hostess fetch us a fresh glass of something else entirely.

Growth is good. Building communities, homes, families, and friendships gives joyful meaning to our lives. Driving our cars to spend time with our friends, e-mailing pictures to extended family, and having dinner out with colleagues are lovely comforts to enjoy. But growth is continuing with no sign of a satisfying ending. How many luxury vehicles will be enough to make us feel content? How many times must we upgrade our electronics? How much is enough?

We have more technology then ever, yet instead of focusing on ways to live more in tune with our natural environment, we have opted to manipulate conditions to suit our personal needs. Too hot? Turn down the air conditioning. House too small? Clear a cornfield and build a bigger one.

Instead of thinking that you must give up all of your comforts and pleasures, I'm suggesting we rethink them, consider the eco-impact, and start looking for more Earth-friendly alternatives. Because the truth is, we can enjoy modern conveniences and contentment *and* take care of Earth. We can forge our own path, make our own list of priorities, and move at a manageable pace. This is an exciting time to become more environmentally active because we can take advantage of so many opportunities.

Let's start by rethinking our consumerism. Right now, we live in a costly cradle-to-grave society. A virgin resource is turned into a new product. The product is used (usually only once), and then it "dies" and ends up as trash. By shifting our belief system and changing our actions, we can move toward a cradle-to-cradle society where virgin products are used, reused, recycled, and reused again. We can close the circle of waste and get more bang for our environmental buck. When we look at the opportunities of reusing and recycling, it's hard not to get excited about what a delightful home we could build. We have the potential to fill our homes with only beautiful and useful products. The first step in making that transition happens with reducing.

The goal of the following three chapters is to put "Reduce, Reuse, and Recycle" into practice. We begin this three-step plan by rethinking our approach to consumerism. We want to use less (reduce), use better (reuse), and use again (recycle). Instead of occasionally practicing the 3R's, we can reprogram our thinking to live these practices. We begin making this transition by taking small, positive eco-actions that result in more environmentally friendly living. Reducing is the first eco-friendly step to focus on as the less we actually consume, the less our overall impact on the environment.

Neither Paper nor Plastic Bags

When friends found out I was writing this book, the first thing they wanted to know was, paper or plastic? Wanting to make better choices at the checkout counter is a great way to go green; however, both paper and plastic have environmental drawbacks.

Plastic bags are made with petroleum and natural gas, two limited natural resources, while paper bags are made from tree pulp, a renewable natural resource, but one whose demands far outweigh its growth. The best answer, therefore, is bringing your own bag. But knowing the rationale behind this decision can help motivate you to make sure you do it.

If you choose to reduce only one thing in your household, let it be plastic bags. These convenient addictions are an ecological nightmare. Although they have existed for only about 30 years, they have become a staple of our society. Environmental groups estimate that more than 500 billion bags will be used throughout the world—this year. That's roughly 60 million tons of oil; yes, oil. Plastic bags are made from petroleum. Meeting our plastic bag needs is further contributing to our energy crisis. Why are so many bags in circulation? Since plastic bags are "free," retailers give consumers more than are needed. I have been guilty of taking one small item out of the store in a plastic bag; an item that could have easily been carried. Shoppers also tend to take more than they need, grabbing two bags when one would do or taking a bag even if they don't need it. I have also been guilty of walking from the deli counter to a table to eat and using a plastic bag to carry my items ten feet! In reality, though, businesses pass on the cost of this convenience to their patrons, and consumers end up paying for the bags anyway. And given that we think they're free, we place little value on them, assuming (rightly so) that we'll just get more next time.

We cannot even depend on bag recycling to answer our plastics problem; this type of recycling is one of the least profitable. Remember, it costs time, energy, money, and resources to recycle, too; and with such a small profit margin, recycling companies are not actively pursuing it. According to www.reusablebags.com, only 1 to 3 percent of plastic bags are recycled. While it's likely that you will reuse a grocery bag once—as a trash can liner, when walking a pet, for a school lunch—the end result is, it will wind up in a landfill. Plastic doesn't biodegrade—it photodegrades, leaching toxins into our environment—so these bags will always be a part of our landscape; they'll take up to a thousand years to fully decompose in landfills. If they're incinerated, they'll release deadly toxins into the air.

Perhaps even worse are the bags that are left to blow in the breeze. Plastic bag litter is not only an eyesore, wreaking havoc on the landscape, but it's also a danger to wildlife. Marine groups like The Ocean Conservancy have found that sea turtles and whales are mistaking the bags as food. After the bags are ingested, the animals' digestive systems are compromised and the animals can die. And don't assume that throwing out a bag you find littering the landscape will mean it biodegrades. In today's modern landfills, decomposition isn't happening. For a product to decompose, it needs an optimal setting of moisture, light, and air. Due to the strict health regulations necessary because of landfill overcrowding, these conditions are a thing of the past. Don't depend on decomposition for paper bags or plastic bags (which photodegrade): bring your own reusable bag and reduce waste altogether.

Plastic bags are suffocating our landfills, threatening our marine life, creating litter, and wasting resources. If this information has you determined to refuse plastic the next time you shop, consider the problems when you ask for paper.

According to the nonprofit organization Californians Against Waste, it takes four times more energy to manufacture a paper bag than a plastic one. Paper bags generate 70 percent more air pollutants than plastic. And although they're made from tree pulp, a renewable resource, tree demands are far outweighing tree growth. With only 10 to 15 percent of paper bags being recycled, we are again depleting natural resources and polluting our environment for a one-time-use disposable product.

While plastic bags are the worst eco-offender, paper bags aren't the answer. So what is?

B.Y.O.B.—bring your own bag. The only real solution to the wasteful practice of plastic and paper bags is to eliminate them. The good news is, this is easy to do!

Many supermarkets have begun selling economically priced, reusable bags and giving you a credit back every time you use them. In our local market, we get "paid" 1¢ for every bag we use. Since my bags cost only 99¢ each, this is an economical way to make a considerable environmental difference. I have gotten accustomed to using these bags on all of my shopping trips, not just at the supermarket, further reducing my reliance on plastic bags.

The biggest problem with using your own bags is actually remembering to use them. Here are some ideas:

Write "remember bags" on the top of your grocery list. I always check my list before I head out the door, to make any last-minute additions, and this reminder really works for me.

Delegate, and turn it into a teaching moment. Put one of your children in charge of remembering the bags, or get in the habit of holding the bag's handles instead of holding hands, and your child will be more likely to remind you to grab one when you get to the store.

Consolidate. After you unpack your groceries, fold all your bags into one and put them back in the car. At the very least, hang them on your coat hook so the next time you're going out, they go with you.

Keep an extra bag on hand in your purse, backpack, or briefcase so you have a bag in a hurry. The Acme Workhorse Style 1500 folds up into a 2"×3"×2" pouch, but when open, can hold over 25 pounds. It's available at www.reusablebags.com.

And, for emergencies, the handy cardboard box. We keep one in our trunk and drop off our purchases between stores. This means less lugging around and another chance to use one of our own bags.

Five-Minute Makeover

The next time your child has a birthday party present to wrap, wrap it up in a reusable bag. Most craft stores sell canvas bags that can be decorated with the recipient's name using fabric paint or markers. Place the gift inside, attach a bow, and give a gift to the birthday child and the earth.

Yes, it will take some time for you to get used to bringing your own bag, and chances are, you'll still use paper or plastic bags every once in awhile. But making a commitment to reduce your dependence on disposable bags will immediately make you a better friend to the trees, the air, the earth, and the sea turtles. And who wouldn't want that?

It's in the Mail

When it comes to waste in the United States, paper is at the top of the list. According to the Environmental Protection Agency, paper and paperboard account for over 35 percent of the waste materials discarded in the country. And one of the biggest offenders of paper waste has your name written all over it: mail. The EPA estimates that out of the 5.5 million tons of mail shipped, over 4 million of it ends up in the garbage. Today you can take a step toward lowering that amount by taking charge of your mailbox.

How many times have you sorted though your day's mail and found only a pile of unwanted credit card solicitations, supermarket flyers, and catalogs? The best course of action for this wasteful practice is to stop it in its tracks. The following contacts can help you do just that:

- Stop credit card solicitations. Help stop the nearly three billion credit card solicitations that are mailed annually by visiting www.optoutprescreen.com. Experian, TransUnion, and Equifax, the country's three major credit-checking agencies, have united to create an official service where consumers can choose to be removed from credit and insurance solicitations. Follow the opt-out prompt, fill in your name and address, and be permanently removed from these mail-ins. If you're concerned about giving out your Social Security number, one of the requests, skip that line; the form is accepted without the information. A confirmation request immediately appears onscreen. Choose to save it on your computer instead of printing it.

- ADVO, Inc., is a leading circular distribution company whose mission is to link retailers with potential customers. While their aim is to service retailers, they also encourage consumers who do not want to receive such mailings to contact them at 1-888-241-6760 where you can decline to receive mailings. You will be connected with an operator who will inform you that it will take four to six weeks to be removed from all lists. Quick and painless. And do Earth an extra favor by declining a mailed confirmation card. Every piece of saved paper counts.

- If you receive Valpak Savings envelopes that you never use, choose to save the paper instead by visiting www.coxtarget.com. Follow the link to the Contact Us page to the mailing list removal list form. Fill in the information exactly as it appears on your mailer and submit it.

- Remove yourself from catalog and other direct-mailing lists by writing to Mail Preference Service, c/o The DMA, P.O. Box 9008 Farmingdale, NY 11735-9008; include in your request your name as it appears on catalogs. Again, it can take four to six weeks for your request to catch up with a company's mailing schedule. If you still want to receive a particular store or company's catalog, contact them directly and request that they not share your information with anyone. Better yet, bookmark the online site and order from a paperless catalog.

Stop unnecessary paper production by contacting these organizations and removing your name and address from their lists. This is an easy activity for teens to take on for you, providing them with a low-maintenance green opportunity that's high on the Earth-friendly scale.

Steer Clear of Hazardous Driving Conditions

No serious conversation can be had about reducing our damaging impact on the environment without discussing cars. According to the Environmental Defense, there are over 239 million cars and light trucks on our roads. Americans make up only 5 percent of the world's population, yet we're responsible for 45 percent of the world's global-warming pollution from vehicles. We need to look at raising our green driving standards.

In a not-too-distant past, airbags and side impact safety features were a luxury, not a manufacturing responsibility. Today our standards have changed and we expect safer cars. It's my hope that this will happen with greener cars. No longer will low-emissions vehicles be out of our price range or considered a luxury "feature." Green cars could be a new standard that includes greater gas mileage in all driving conditions and lower emissions. But you don't have to wait for this to happen to make a positive emissions change.

Regardless of your car's make or model, driving more efficiently is a responsible practice all motorists can get behind when we get behind the wheel. Let's start with something we should all be doing anyway: obeying the speed limit. Not only is it the law and a safety matter, but it's an environmental issue. Aggressive driving, sudden braking, and rapid acceleration put unnecessary stress on your engine and Earth. According to www.fueleconomy.gov, aggressive driving can cost you more money at the pump. Driving just 5 mph over the 60 mph speed limit increases your gas cost by 20 cents per gallon. We can help decrease our dependence on foreign oil and reduce wasteful carbon emissions by abiding by the laws designed to keep us safe.

Keys to Greener Driving

Turn off your car and turn down your emissions instead of idling. When a car idles, you get 0 miles to the gallon but are still emitting toxic chemicals into the air. It's a lose, lose scenario. If your children ride the school bus, be sure to check the idling procedures when buses are parked outside the building before afternoon dismissal. Ask where the building intake vents are and make sure that the bus parking lot is not located in that area, or your children could be inhaling an additional 40 toxic chemicals from diesel fuel emissions. If you find a problem, request that the bus parking lot be changed or that the vehicles commit to a "no idling policy."

When using your car for weekend errands, save time, energy, and the environment by effectively planning your work week. Designate shopping days and plan for an extended afternoon when you can hit several stores in one day instead of spreading your trips over the course of several days. A warm engine is the most efficient. Moving from one store to the next on a preplanned route can save you about half the amount of gas it would take to keep restarting your errands from home on different days. During the work week, look into telecommuting and avoiding the car altogether, carpooling to reduce your personal carbon emissions, or driving during off-peak hours to avoid fuel waste and idling. If possible in your area, try using public transportation. Even opting for a ride once a week can make a difference, giving you, your car, and the air a much needed rest.

The better care we take of the things we own, the longer we can go before having to replace them. Motor oil is the lifeblood of your car and plays a critical part in your automobile's efficiency. If you don't already do it, take care of your engine by providing it with the manufacturer's recommended grade of oil, and you'll improve your gas mileage 1 to 2 percent. Manufacturers and mechanics recommend changing your oil anyway from 3,000 to 10,000 miles. If you're a conservative driver who obeys speed limits and doesn't drive aggressively, an oil change at 5,000 miles is a good rule of thumb. If you drive in extreme weather conditions, tow heavy loads, or drive like you're a NASCAR contender, you should change your oil more frequently. Changing your oil is important because oil breaks down due to high temperatures and loses its effectiveness as a lubricant, or it builds up with dust and by-products and can corrode the engine. Both scenarios can cause costly engine problems.

When taking your car in for an oil change, ask your mechanic about the shop's recycling procedures. Used oil can be recycled and used for new products, burned for energy, or used to generate electricity. Since oil doesn't wear out, it can be properly cleaned, recycled, and re-refined into lubricating motor oils that meet all the criteria of new motor oils. Reusing oil means less dependence on foreign oil and less strain on our resources, since recycling oil uses less energy than manufacturing new oil. If you're changing your oil yourself, be sure to follow recommended safety instructions to avoid spilling oil and damaging our land and water. Take used oil, and used oil filters, to a recycling plant or a mechanic who can recycle it properly. Never pour oil down the drain or into the sewer, as it can contaminate the land and water. When choosing a re-refined oil, The American Automobile Manufacturers Association has teamed with the American Petroleum Institute and issued a certification mark for re-refined oils which signifies it is a high-quality motor oil. The "sunburst" designation means the re-refined oil has met the same strict standards of nonrecycled oil.

It's Easy Driving Green

Responsible driving is more then following the rules of the road; it's about making environmentally sound decisions with your driving. You need not put off eco-friendly driving until you're ready to buy a new car, nor should you be the only driver navigating a greener road. Since teens love their cars and we want them to love the environment, let's help them to do both. Teach your teen some rules of the eco-friendly road and help raise a more conscientious driver with these easy-to-implement ideas:

Avoid "treating" your car to a higher octane than it really needs. That can actually do more harm than good, as most experts agree that higher octane fuels create more pollution. The EPA states that "unless your car needs high-octane gasoline, use of 'premium' gas will not improve performance or emissions—it will just cost you more."

Don't top off your tank when filling up at the pump. The auto experts at www.cars.com caution that an overfilled tank prevents toxic vapors from being properly contained in the recovery canister. These vapors can escape into the atmosphere, creating ground level smog and air pollution.

Look for those black "accordion" covers at the pump. Whenever possible, fill up at a pump that has one of these covers on the nozzle. They're vapor-recovery devices that collect toxic fumes.

Park your car in the shade. That will limit gas evaporation and keep your interior cooler, which will help you limit air-conditioning in warm weather. If you have a garage, using it can lessen your need to warm up your car on cold mornings or cool it down on hot afternoons. Skipping the air-conditioning in favor of fresh air lowers gas needs and limits the environmentally unfriendly chemicals needed to run it.

Pack wisely when heading out on a road trip. Avoid using the roof rack; it creates drag, which will cause your car to use more fuel. And unpack as soon as you arrive. Lightening your load by 100 pounds can save you up to 2 percent in gas mileage.

Avoid traveling at peak times. Stop-and-go traffic leads to the lowest fuel efficiency. If the air conditioner is on during rush-hour delays, your fuel efficiency can decrease by as much as 12 percent. If possible, give your car and yourself a break from the daily driving grind and speak to the home office about flextime options or telecommuting.

Making more responsible driving decisions with your current car will have a positive eco-impact and could inspire you to consider even more eco-alternatives when it's time to choose your next ride. When shopping for your next automobile, make sure it comes in your favorite color: green, of course! Look for models that are eco-friendly, that suit your driving needs, and that match your financial goals.

A hybrid car is powered by two different sources: an internal combustion engine—which you are probably used to driving now—that operates on fuel, and an electric system. These cars produce less greenhouse gases like carbon dioxide and carbon monoxide, making them more environmentally desirable. Currently, a hybrid car is most efficient in city driving, where constant stopping and starting triggers the electric system and saves gas. If you live in the country or do a lot of highway driving, you won't benefit from hybrid driving. In fact, you could end up with worse fuel efficiency than with a conventional car, a common complaint with some hybrid car owners.

So which car is the right choice for you? Knowing your transportation needs and researching the possibilities is your best bet. A good place to start is www.greenercars.org, the official website of the American Council for an Energy Efficient Economy. This site rates all cars, not just hybrids, and organizes findings based on model and class, with a fast-find section highlighting the best and worst of previous years. There's also a resource page with links to all major automakers and organizations of environmental interest. But no matter which type of car you choose to buy, driving responsibly puts you on the road to greener living.

Reduce Personal Toxins

Perhaps one of the most important things we can do on our quest to reduce our stress on the environment is to reduce our own stress. Feeling overworked and underappreciated is a recipe for eco-trouble. Tired minds make tired decisions. You're much more likely to throw up your hands and throw plastics in the garbage, hit Print when you're already holding a copy, forget your cloth bags in the car, and leave the lights on if you're mind is elsewhere. Learning to take better care of ourselves goes hand in eco-hand with learning to take better care of Earth.

Time management is not learned overnight. Our busy schedules often force us to fit too many hours of activity into an already exhausted calendar. We rush from place to place, never really taking time to enjoy who we're with or look forward to where we're going. Life becomes a series of "to-do" lists with not enough check marks on them. Prioritizing our time is a gift we can give to ourselves, our families, and our planet.

With your family nearby, get a bird's-eye view of the upcoming week. I encourage sitting together with a calendar, Blackberry, and school agenda. If your teens complain that they're too busy to tell you what they have on their schedule, explain that if something isn't on the family calendar, there's no guarantee it will get done. "Forgetting" to leave your teen the car keys so she can get to softball practice on time may be just the friendly lesson she needs to bring her to the family meeting next time.

Fill in the family calendar—a reusable wipe board works really well—giving everyone a chance to share plans. Then prioritize the top three activities of the week. Music recital? Doctor's appointment? Whatever the occasion, denote the significance of the activity with a star and make a commitment to saying no to any and all other invitations or activities that may come up on that day. A friend needs a ride home from school? Grandma wants to stop by? On those days, no additional events are to be added. Prioritizing your week and setting limits are wonderful ways to begin to learn boundaries. Just as we're used to taking more than we need when it comes to natural resources (extra-long showers, air-conditioning in an empty house), we're used to taking on more than we can comfortably handle. Learning to set limits in our personal lives will translate to setting limits in our environmental lives.

Five-Minute Makeover

Take five minutes for yourself each day. Sit with a cup of tea or a glass of ice water and put your feet up. We can be so busy taking care of everyone and everything else that we forget about ourselves. Rejuvenate yourself.

I've talked about reducing waste in terms of garbage. Now we want to add to that commitment a plan to reduce wasting our time, as haste makes waste. Once we begin to better manage our daily schedules, we can take time to do things right the first time. Imagine all the spilled milk, oil, and water that we could save if we weren't rushing. Wasteful practices add up. Staying fresh and focused helps avoid waste. And instead of rewarding yourself for a job well done with a sugary treat, try giving yourself a full night's rest. Instead of unwinding in front of the television, try taking a 10-minute walk. A clear head and healthy body contribute to clearer thinking and cleaner living.

Once you and the children clear away extraneous commitments and your family is left with more time, doing the activities that you all enjoy and exploring ideas from your eco-calendar will fast find their way into your routine. But if completing less-than-desirable chores is taking up too much of your time, consider a little time-waste management in this area, too. When we don't like what we're doing, we tend to spend more time doing it than necessary, which is peculiar since we don't want to be doing it at all. Consider how many times you've heard your kids whine about not wanting to do something, watched as they sluggishly prolong the chore, and then reprimanded them for doing a poor job. Efficiency is earth-friendly. Help your whole family use their own energy more efficiently by setting a timer for 10 minutes when chores loom large. Having a starting and stopping point can make the task feel more manageable, greatly increasing the chance that it will be done right, in the right amount of time.

We can further reduce personal wasteful practices by choosing only what we need, instead of what we want. An easy way to begin making the transition from want to need happens when we measure what we have on hand. For example, how many times have you stood in front of your closet, filled with sweaters, jeans, and accessories, and said, "I have nothing to wear"? Before heading to the store and buying an entirely new outfit, look at new ways to pair old staples. By taking a few minutes to consider what you already have on hand, you could end up opting for a new accessory over a new wardrobe.

You can use the same idea in the kitchen. Before heading to the store and stocking up on ingredients you may already have, look over your current inventory. Instead of calling for takeout or making an isolated drive to the supermarket, use the food you have on hand to whip up a light dinner.

The following quotes on simplicity are useful to write down and post in high-traffic areas like the closet or fridge as a reminder that having more is not always necessary. Filling a home with beautiful and useful items, instead of merely cluttering it up with "things," is an act of eco-reverence. Consider the following quotes as you transition from consumer to reducer:

Go confidently in the direction of your dreams! Live the life you've imagined. As you simplify your life, the laws of the universe will be simpler.

—Henry David Thoreau

Our life is frittered away by detail …. Simplify, simplify, simplify!

—Henry David Thoreau

Life is really simple, but we insist on making it complicated.

—Confucius

Simplicity is making the journey of this life with just baggage enough.

—Author Unknown

I believe that a simple and unassuming manner of life is best for everyone, best both for the body and the mind.

—Albert Einstein

Making the simple complicated is commonplace; making the complicated simple, awesomely simple, that's creativity.

—Charles Mingus

Live simply that others might simply live.

—Elizabeth Seaton

Simplicity is the ultimate sophistication.

—Leonardo DaVinci

Who is rich? He who rejoices in his portion.

—The Talmud

Be content with what you have, rejoice in the way things are. When you realize there is nothing lacking, the whole world belongs to you.

—Lao Tzu

Simplicity, clarity, singleness: these are the attributes that give our lives power and vividness and joy.

—Richard Halloway

The sculptor produces the beautiful statue by chipping away such parts of the marble block as are not needed—it is a process of elimination.

—Elbert Hubbard

As you began to rethink your actions from an environmental perspective by looking at ways to reduce your impact on natural resources, you're taking meaningful steps to create a more plentiful Earth and a more peaceful household. You'll begin to recover resources and replenish Earth's bounty. You'll be giving it a chance to catch up, to revitalize. You'll say to your hostess, "Let me clean up for you. You've already done so much."

Chapter Checklist

- ☐ We will remember that reducing, reusing, and recycling starts with rethinking.
- ☐ We can and will stop wasteful postal practices.
- ☐ We will bring our own bags to the stores.
- ☐ We can be more eco-friendly with our current car.
- ☐ We will reduce personal stress and clutter, knowing that simple is satisfying.

Reuse: Salvage and Save

Consumer Reports, a nonprofit publication of *Consumers Union*, recently revealed a startling statistic. An investigation found that New York City's Department of Sanitation collects over 700,000 tons of reusable "garbage." A lot of what passes for garbage in most people's homes could be reused in another capacity but is being thrown out. Why does this happen? Because we have been conditioned to think that a product has one purpose only. We have been bombarded with commercials that claim to be selling the new, improved versions of products, many of which are "disposable" for our *convenience*. Once we finish with them, they're done, and it's back to the store for more stuff. As an eco-friendly family, you can stop that resource-robbing trend in its tracks.

Back to Basics

There was a time when consumers valued quality and longevity in their purchases. We looked for items that would "stand the test of time" or "take a licking and keep on ticking." The idea of replacing big-ticket items like televisions, furniture, and dishes was unheard of. In fact, even lower-end items like coffee mugs, children's bicycles, and "freebies" like the aluminum foil used to wrap leftover food at a restaurant were treated with care. Consumers repaired belongings rather than assuming they would just get a new one; a kind of attention to detail used to be regarded as frugal, favored by the Depression-era generation who knew what it was like to go without. Thankfully, with our perspectives turning a brighter shade of green, we know that extending the longevity of our consumable goods is not only frugal, it is environmentally friendly. Learning to reuse purchases is good for the earth, financially beneficial, and fun for the whole family.

As we learn how and where we can reduce our eco-impact, we'll also be taking better care of the things we choose to own. Knowing that we can extend the life of a purchase by using it in more ways is an excellent motivation for treating items with greater respect. Reusing happens in two basic ways: we either use the item again for its original function or we look at the item from a new perspective and find a new use for it. Whether you choose to focus on a conventional approach and reuse your glass jars for food storage or try something new, like filling those jars with homemade bath salts and giving them away as gifts, the advantageous results are the same: fewer raw resources needed, less energy used, and a lengthier life achieved.

Five-Minute Makeover

Eco-friendly organizations in New York City are working hard to make a difference in waste management. Programs like Materials for the Arts (www.mfta.org) and Tools for Schools (www.toolsforschoolssolutions.org) work to redistribute everything from office chairs to artwork, to fax machines, to public schools, to community art programs and other nonprofit organizations so they can operate and expand. Committed to preserving natural resources by reusing products, organizations like these can always use your support.

Reusing helps get more bangs for each environmental buck. Having already expended the resources to turn raw material into a purchased product, we want to get as much use out of it as we can. Remember, we want to live in a cradle-to-cradle society, where everything is used and reused until it is worn-out or broken, at which point it is recycled. A great place to start reusing is with items that have multiple purposes.

When you think about it, just about everything can be used and reused again. Even paper towel rolls can be of further use when we rethink the possibilities. A paper towel holder holds paper towels, yes—but it can also store rolled-up art projects, prevent Christmas lights from becoming tangled, or be decorated and cut into smaller pieces and then used as homemade napkin rings. From now on, we can rethink our purchases and change our consumer mantra from "I need another one" to "Once is not enough."

If the idea of creative reducing has you thinking, "Where am I supposed to store all of these containers? How can I find the time? I'm not creative," relax. As I've said before, we are transitioning to greener living. It doesn't happen overnight. Don't pressure yourself to think that you have to do it all. Pick a project that you feel is manageable and begin there. Over time, you'll put your reusing systems in place and feel better equipped to do more.

Save Resources, Save Green

Financially, choosing to use what you have on hand in lieu of buying new makes good cents. While you may be used to the convenience of going to the store and picking up what you need, this chapter helps you redefine what "need" really means. For instance, you may think you "need" a plastic desk organizer to keep track of pens, ruler, and thumbtacks. What you really "need" are containers to store your supplies. Aluminum cans washed, dried, and decorated can do just that. As we did in the previous chapter, we want to rethink our needs with an eye toward limiting environmentally unfriendly practices.

One of the biggest benefits of your new reducing practice will be the emphasis on family fun. There's no mistaking any of the ideas in this chapter for chores. Once you start creating, crafting, and changing your ideas about trash and treasures, you'll find you've tapped into a wealth of creativity that has been waiting for an effective outlet. You'll be pleasantly surprised to find that you don't need to buy craft items; you already have a slew of supplies on hand. Instead of having to make a trip to the store to buy entertaining activities to keep the kids occupied, you can save time, money, and energy making something new out of something old.

Put Your Green Foot Forward

Regardless of where you choose to live, there's always one person who makes no qualms about moving in: the sock monster. Laundry rooms all across the country have bags, baskets, or bunches of mismatched socks; the sock monster has snatched up all the mates and dragged them to his lair. In all likelihood, you'll never see them again; the sock monster never asks for a ransom.

This phenomenon of disappearing socks, which used to be such an annoyance, can actually be a wonderful way to practice reusing. Since we all have these items on hand, and may even have a designated area to keep them, they provide a perfect opportunity for rethinking and reusing. Reconsider how useful your mismatched socks really are with ideas and inspirations the whole family can enjoy.

Simple Sock Projects

- Baby socks are wonderful for collecting those last slivers of soap. A soap-dispensing sock can be a great washcloth for kids.
- Save the baby socks you still have paired by washing them in one of Mom or Dad's socks. They'll get cleaned without getting separated.
- Use a baby sock as a scented sachet and get rid of sneaker odor. Put a heaping tablespoon of baking soda into the sock and stuff it in the toe of an offending shoe. Remove it in the morning.
- Find soothing relief from an old sock by filling it with rice, tying a knot at the end, and microwaving it for one minute. Apply it to aches and pains.
- Cut the top off an old tube sock and use it as a cute "tube dress" for a doll. Add embellishments with miscellaneous buttons, sequins, or ribbon pieces.

- The top of a tube sock can also make a great drink cozy for cold cans of soda.

- Sock puppets never go out of style and are a great way to reuse old buttons and leftover pieces of yarn.

- Make a sock snowman by filling a long sock with beans and tying a knot at the end. Put rubber bands one third of the way up, creating the base, and a third of the way up from the bottom to separate the middle and top snowballs. Decorate and enjoy.

- Cover a broom handle with a long sock secured with a rubber band, and use it to clean hard-to-reach places like your dryer's lint trap, under the fridge, and behind the washer.

Five-Minute Makeover

Practice approaching your recyclables from a fresh perspective by filling in these blanks:

A toddler could reuse a coffee can by _____.

A grade schooler could reuse a glass jar by _____.

A tween could reuse a milk carton by _____.

A teen could reuse broken crayons by _____.

You'll find more suggestions for these things throughout the chapter.

Your mismatched socks have a lot more uses than you've probably ever considered. But once you start looking at what you own from an environmental perspective, everything can have greater potential. Before you throw something into the recycling container, remember the Sock Project and take a moment to consider what other tasks the item in your hands could be reused for.

The Art of Reusing

You can also start to look at two old objects as the ingredients to create a new one. Partnering reusable items can lead to even more new creations. For instance, every house I know has broken crayons, usually rolling around the bottom of a toy box. How often have we found one of these leftovers and mindlessly thrown it away? Instead of becoming frustrated at more money, and resources, down the drain, try a family-friendly art project that rids the house of leftover crayon clutter while producing a new and useful item that kids will love to make.

Crayon Cupcakes

1. Send children out to gather all old and broken crayon pieces throughout the house, the backseat of the car, and the bottom of your purse.
2. Peel away any leftover paper.
3. Break crayons into smaller pieces.
4. Using an old muffin tray, fill muffin tins with crayon pieces.
5. Bake at 300°F for approximately five minutes, or until wax melts.
6. Let cool overnight.
7. Remove new crayon creations! These crayons make beautiful leaf rubbings.

If you have a teen who would scoff at such a baby activity, try taking a more "mature" (meaning, money-making) approach and adjust the project accordingly.

Candy Crayons

1. Follow steps 1 through 3.
2. Place crayon chunks in a glass measuring cup and microwave in 15-second increments, stirring gently in between, until crayons are melted and run together.
3. Pour crayon mix into plastic holiday candy molds (saved from last season) and insert a "candy stick."
4. Let cool overnight.

5. Sell these Candy Crayons at a local craft fair to make holiday money.

As parents, we can all too quickly think, "My kids are too old for that." But by taking a simple kiddy activity and, again, rethinking it, we can often find a grown-up equivalent. Of course, the more often you practice being a reuser, and the more often your teens see the benefits of their efforts, the easier it will be to get these reluctant environmentalists on board. There's no age limit to reusing your recyclables, nor are there any rules. The most important thing is to find a second (and third and fourth) use for the items you have already environmentally invested in. You can also use eco-ideas as an excellent opportunity to spend more time with your kids.

Egg-cellent Eco-Ideas

Eggs are a staple in our family's diet, and as such we tend to accumulate egg cartons. While our local health food stores welcomes the return of our cartons, we have found that these items are tailor-made for fun family activities. From toddlers to teens, we have used egg cartons to busy ourselves on a rainy day and turned them into handmade holiday gifts. Here's one cardboard egg carton reused four different ways:

1. **Toddler**—Create an egg carton caterpillar in the spring. Cut the top part off the egg carton, and then cut between the two egg holder rows. Paint each row and let dry. Insert pipe cleaners for legs and decorate with craft scraps like button eyes. Glue grass onto the inside of the top of the container and display your many-legged friends.

2. **Grade schooler**—Play homemade Memory. Using miscellaneous items like paper clips, erasers, pen caps, and crayons, fill each egg hole with one item. Have your child turn around and remove an item. See if he can remember what is missing. Make the game more difficult by removing two items and rearranging the remaining pieces while your child looks away.

3. **Tween**—Give a Golf Ball Caddy gift. Paint an entire egg carton a favorite color. Embellish it with the recipient's name and decorate it with stickers and other craft materials. Fill the egg holes with old Easter basket grass, and place new golf balls "on the green."

4. **Teens**—Make an Off-Limits Organizer. Is there anything worse for a teen than a sibling touching his stuff? Keep small, important items like jewelry, iPod earphones, and spare keys well organized and out of reach from curious hands. Paint and decorate carton as desired. Fill egg carton with personal items and slip a rubber band around both sides of the carton to keep it closed or tie it closed with coordinating ribbon.

Five-Minute Makeover

Looking for a fun and fast family game night? Split the family into teams and give each a cardboard box, recyclable containers, and a roll of duct tape. The challenge is to build one of the following: a life-saving device, equipment for a new sports game, a new fashion trend, and so on. The possibilities can last as long as you want.

Tween and Teen Scenes

If the idea of eco-fun with your tweens and teens seems like a far-fetched dream, let me assure you, it isn't. Your super-social, too-cool kids have a confession to make: they want to spend more time with you. Not on Friday night, when everyone's going to the game, and not at the bus stop, where everyone is looking, but they do want more of your attention. In writing this book, I spoke with many young adults who loved the idea of making things like crafts and gifts; who thought spending one-on-one time with a parent would be so fun; and who, throughout our conversation, became genuinely interested in making a difference in their home, community, and world. Yes, you will have to get the ball rolling, and your great green ideas may be met with some initial eye-rolling, but sometimes we teach our kids to be suspicious of us. We can be so busy at times; when was the last time you and your teens sat down for some "no-strings-attached" family fun?

If your environmental efforts aren't taking root, try to find another motivation for reusing what's on hand. Moving away from the "new is better" mentality is especially difficult with teens; just consider how many advertising dollars are put toward targeting them. If we want to get our teens on board with living more in tune with nature, we need to come up with ideas that work for them.

Almost all teens need to show some kind of community activity on their resumé. From college transcripts to summer jobs, administrators and employers appreciate a solid letter of recommendation. If your teen thinks saving yogurt cups is a waste of time, give him an opportunity to think outside of the recycling box. Collecting reusable items for a local organization and teaching participants how to better reuse the items is an inexpensive and environmentally friendly way to meet community service requirements.

Preschools, vacation Bible schools, day camps, and scout troop meetings use a myriad of supplies to complete projects. Connecting with one of these groups is a low-maintenance way to get involved in an eco-activity. Reach out to neighbors with younger children or friends of the family to find out what activities they are involved in and whether a donation could help. In the spring, a scout troop would surely appreciate learning how two dozen clean yogurt cups could be used for planting seedlings, while a preschool may welcome a box full of egg cartons, and a guest teacher, for its art class. If your teens are reluctant to turn something old into something new, help them become the connection for an organization that depends on community generosity to thrive.

If your tween has exceptionally good organizational skills, he may want to help everyone else in the house green up their act. How many times have you bought another stick of glue only to find yours in the drawer when you got home? Gather up miscellaneous supplies like loose pens, tape, rulers, paper clips, and the like, and have your tween organize "office stations" throughout the house. While these mismatched supplies may not be "suitable" for school, they don't have to be banished to the back of the drawer or, worse yet, thrown away. You can reuse last year's school supplies at home.

The Nine Lives of Cans and Jars

Chances are, you have coffee cans and glass jars on hand, but you've been recycling them. While recycling is a much better alternative to the trash, reusing items before recycling is ideal. If you're worried about cluttering your pantry with a ton of miscellaneous recyclables, I suggest focusing on these two gems and adding to your reusing routine as you see fit. Once you begin to see all the advantages of keeping containers like these around, it won't be long before you're rethinking all of your recycle bales! A reinvestment with these investments is so advantageous because they have numerous purposes.

Aluminum Coffee Cans

Once you've emptied the contents, breathe new life into that old can with these tips and tricks:

- **Make music**—Cover cans with construction paper and decorate. Fill with rice or beans and shake, shake, shake; or tie two cans together with twine, then make a loop to carry the set. Use wooden spoons and march to your own beat.

- **Make monster feet**—Flip over two cans, then drill two holes on either side. Lace a piece of sturdy twine through the holes, long enough for a child to stand on top of the cans and hold the ends of the twine. Have your own monster mash.

- **Keep organized**—Fill coffee can with pens, pencils, and recycled scrap paper. Set one near the telephone for message taking.

- **Make a meal**—Lightly flour the outside of the can. Flatten pizza dough using the can as a roller. Use the bottom of the can to "cut out" mini-pizzas that each child can top with his favorite ingredients.

- **... or a flower vase**—Cover and decorate the outside of the can, fill it with water, and arrange fresh-cut flowers inside.

- **... or toys**—Empty cans make excellent toys for the sandbox or water table.

- **... or mini-golf holes**—Fill cans with a few scoops of sand or a couple of large rocks to weigh them down when they're on their side. Arrange cans throughout the lawn and play golf.

- **... or memory keepers**—Take cans along on a trail walk and collect leaves, rocks, and flowers.

- **... or a cookie jar**—Bake a batch of cookies and deliver them in a decorated coffee can. Attach a note with all the ideas you have for reusing the can after the cookies have been enjoyed, and share your eco-spirit.

🌀 **... or floor hockey**—Gather two empty coffee cans for "goals," use the plastic lids as "sticks," and find a small ball to use as the "puck." Try to score goals on your opponent by using a lid to hit the ball into the can. Great game for siblings!

Glass Jars

With such an assortment of shapes and sizes to reuse, it's a wonder glass jars are ever recycled. Collect several bottles and remove their labels by soaking them in warm, soapy water for about an hour. For stuck-on pieces, rub olive oil on the area and use a credit card to lift the stubborn remnants.

Food storage. Glass jars can be cleaned and sterilized in your dishwasher and then used again to keep food fresh.

Tools of the trade. Help Dad organize his workshop by nailing the lids of baby jars to the bottom of a piece of wood. Hang the wood just above eye level. Fill the jars with washers, nails, and bits, and then screw the jars into the lids.

Glove drier. Set jars by the door where wet and cold snow lovers come in, and have each family member cover a jar with a glove for fast air-drying. Baby food jars work great for mittens, while sauce jars are good for adult gloves.

Potpourri gift. Poke holes in a baby jar lid, then fill the jar with potpourri. Screw on the top and cover it with a thin piece of colorful fabric or a decorative doily, which you can keep in place with a rubber band that you cover with a matching ribbon. Place it in the bathroom.

Candleholders. Fill large glass jars one quarter full with play sand. Decorate the outside with puffy paint or stickers. Insert a small votive candle inside.

Terrarium. Wash and dry a large glass jar. Fill the bottom with a handful of gravel (for drainage) and a handful of charcoal chips (for odor; available at a garden nursery). Using a large kitchen spoon, add several scoops of high-quality potting soil. Add a humidity-loving plant like moss, and decorate with small shells and rocks. Spritz with water to make the environment moist, not drenched. After a few days in dim light, move it to brighter—but not direct—light and enjoy your indoor garden.

Collect bugs. Punch holes in the lid of a large glass jar and place a handful of grass inside. Collect lightning bugs at twilight, place them inside the jar, and watch them light up. Be sure to let them go at the end of the night!

Make a snowglobe. Use a hot glue gun or epoxy to fasten small decorations, like discarded dollhouse toys, to the inside lid of a baby food jar. Fill the jar with water, 1/2 teaspoon glitter, and three drops of glycerin (available at craft stores). When the glue dries, screw on the top cover with coordinating fabric and a rubber band, shake, turn over, and display.

The beauty of reusing your own containers is that there are no rules. Activities and ideas can grow and mature with your children. If you read those suggestions with a teenager in mind, you'll want to give her more room for individual design. Coffee cans can also be painted, decoupaged, and glued together to make containers for accessories. Large glass jars can be ornately decorated and used as candleholders, while baby food jars can become keepsake snowglobe mementos displaying vacation memories.

Since teens favor spending time with their friends, you may consider hosting a present-making party where guests can make a gift to give. As the holidays approach, invite friends over to assemble homemade "Cookie Jars." Instead of baking the actual cookies, kids can organize the ingredients and give the gift to someone they know could benefit from a special visit. From grandparents to younger siblings, giving the gift of time is made even sweeter with these treats!

Homemade Cookie Jars

Using a glass quart jar, design the perfect "layer cookie" with these step-by-step directions:

1. Combine 3/4 cup all-purpose flour, 1 teaspoon baking soda, and 1/2 teaspoon salt, and pour into jar.
2. Layer 1 cup mini chocolate chips on top of flour.
3. Layer 3/4 cup firmly packed brown sugar on top of chips.
4. Layer 1/2 cup chopped walnuts on top of sugar.
5. Layer 1 1/4 cups uncooked quick oats on top of walnuts.
6. Sprinkle cinnamon on top.

7. Screw on lid tightly and top with decorative fabric. Attach recipe card.

8. Recipe card: Preheat oven to 350°F.

   In large bowl, mix one large egg (slightly beaten), ¾ cup butter, and ½ teaspoon vanilla extract until well blended. Stir in jar contents and mix well. Arrange spoonfuls of dough on greased cookie sheet and bake for 12 to 15 minutes. Makes about 3 dozen cookies.

Holiday How-to

Reusable containers can also be customized to suit every season. Decorating your home with inspired creations is better for the environment and more meaningful. While your child's homemade flower bouquet may never make the front cover of a gift catalog, it will surely hold an important place in your personal memory book.

It is amazing to me how much money we spend on holiday decorations. From high-end ceramic collectibles to plastic reindeer, shopping centers are crammed with expensive seasonal items. Skip the store-bought items and have fun designing your own holiday villages using milk cartons. We go through half-gallon milk containers like, well, milk. We've also used our fair share of orange juice pints and half-pints of heavy cream. These sturdy containers can be reused until the cows come home.

Here are just two holiday ideas:

- **Haunted houses**—Clean and dry a milk carton. Cut out "windows" and a door (cut on three sides so it has a hinge). Cover with dark paint and embellish with cotton ball ghosts and construction paper bats.

- **Santa's workshop**—The same theory as haunted houses, but paint with festive Christmas colors. Add a few drops of water to the last of a glue bottle, dip a paint brush, and "paint" the roof with glue. Sprinkle glitter on top for snow. This craft works well with a spout container. Tug loosely on a cotton ball and stuff it into the spout to represent chimney smoke. If your family uses a host of different containers, consider decorating an entire snow village and display your recycled town on the mantel.

Five-Minute Makeover

Need a fast and fun winter activity? Take a few minutes to gather up the supplies for these ice prisms, and then let nature take its natural chilly course.

Use an old pie tin to collect leaves, pinecones, and acorns. Fill the pan three quarters of the way with water. Place both ends of a strong piece of string in the water so you're left with a loop outside the tin. Place the tin outside to freeze. In the morning, take it out of the tin and hang your winter wonderland prism.

Fresh Ideas for Spring

Greet warmer weather with these two ideas that make the most of your leftovers. Take a cue from nature and create colorful house-warming presents and festive containers to hold them in.

- **Spring flowers**—Collect a dozen used dryer sheets. Lay two sheets on top of one another, pinch the middle, and turn to create a flower bloom. Attach the bloom to a green pipe cleaner. Fill various reusable containers with water and add different food colors to each. Dip flowers in water. Place over the sink to dry. Arrange your bouquet.

- **Flowerpot mosaics**—Take an old chipped dish and break it into little pieces by putting it into a brown paper bag and hitting it with the side of a hammer. Glue pieces onto a terra-cotta pot, leaving space in between each. Let dry. Cover the entire pot with grout, making sure to fill in all the cracks. Let dry. Wipe off excess grout with a damp sponge and fill flowerpot.

Clean Out Your Closet for Good

When you consider items that you can reuse, your children's clothes are probably at the top of the list. Even after you pass down your kids' outfits through the family, give away some favorites to friends, and then give away others to neighbors, you'll probably be left with a dresser filled with clothes. In addition, there are your old business suits, your husband's old T-shirts and jackets, and boots and accessories you no longer need or want. With so many people needing help, clothes should never be thrown out.

The average American throws away over 60 pounds of clothes and rags a year, according to Charity Guide, a nonprofit online site committed to helping people help others. Of all the clothes that end up in landfills, the majority belong to women. This is especially upsetting when you consider how many disadvantaged women could benefit from specialty items like suits, formal wear, and shoes. If we want our children to be eco-friendly, let's be the change we want to see. Stop throwing out your perfectly good clothes and donate to one of these amazing charities. You'll not only be donating your clothes—you'll be donating your support.

Dress for Success is a nonprofit organization committed to helping disadvantaged women suit up for a job interview, giving them a better chance at entering the workforce. Donating to them is an excellent opportunity for you to help women become more self-sufficient. Visit www.dressforsuccess.org for drop-off locations and details.

The Princess Project (www.princessproject.org) and The Glass Slipper Project (www.glassslipperproject.org) both connect young women with formal wear for prom. Visit these sites to learn where they are and how you can be a part of some young woman's once-in-a-lifetime night.

If you aren't sentimentally attached to your wedding gown, you may want to donate it to the Making Memories Breast Cancer Foundation. Their national bridal sales raise money to grant wishes to breast cancer patients and their families. You can find information about the Brides Against Breast Cancer events, grant wishes, and make financial donations at www.makingmemories.org.

When you're finished with your maternity clothes, contact your area Planned Parenthood or women's shelter to see if they'd like these specialty items. Goodwill and the Salvation Army have long been excellent resources when it comes to clothing donations. Contact these organizations to find the nearest clothing collection center.

Five-Minute Makeover

Use your next celebration as a chance to celebrate Earth by opting for these fast and functional ideas.

Having an unusually big party? Call a catering service and inquire about renting serving dishes instead of buying new.

Are the kids in your son's playgroup all turning the same age this year? Consider buying a set of festive decorations to share among families.

Thinking about buying paper and plastics for a get-together at your house? Instead, invite each guest to bring their favorite place setting and enjoy an eco-friendly eclectic table.

Environmentally Friendly Deals

I have to admit, when my first son was born, I wanted all of his toys to be new. I thought that somehow made them better and, by association, made me a better mother. Thankfully, those misconstrued feelings were short-lived, and my second son has hardly ever played with a brand-new toy.

With interests and milestones passing so quickly, there's little reason to consider a new toy a worthy financial or environmental investment. Garage sales are a great place for picking up toys in good condition at great prices. Our town recently hosted a town-wide garage sale to raise money for the Blair Women's Club, a local women's club in our area, and it was great to see so many neighbors finding curbside treasures. I spoke with broker and owner of RE/MAX Ridge Real Estate Gail Masson-Romano, one of the participating merchants whose company provided the signs for the event. Gail is happy to donate her time and energies to a function that helps to unite the community and benefits the environment. Local corporate sponsorship helps to make events like a town-wide garage sale possible, and many merchants welcome the opportunity to connect their business name to such a well-attended occasion.

Here is a brief outline of the way our women's club organized this fund-raising event:

1. Form a committee which includes a contact person for participants who collects fees, a public relations person to solicit business support, a media person for advertising the event, and a project leader to coordinate all of these efforts.

2. Decide on a date.

3. Elect a contact person.

4. Approach local businesses for financial support or other items that could be useful. For instance, RE/MAX Ridge Real Estate donated "open house" signs to the event so shoppers knew to look for consistent markers while following the map.

5. Post flyers inviting homeowners to participate. For a small cost (the suggested fee was $10), homeowners could have their home and the items they would be selling listed on a map that was sold to yard sale shoppers (suggested cost $1).

6. Collect fees; compile names, addresses, and items; and make the map. Make copies.

7. Sell the maps at a high-traffic location, like a local supermarket.

8. Advertise the event in the local paper.

9. Post markers/signs at addresses the night before the event.

10. Enjoy a community event that benefits neighbors and the neighborhood!

Consignment sales are another great place to find reused bargains and to cash in on your gently used merchandise. Laurie Owens, a stay-at-home mother of three, has taken this concept to the next level with her company, Kidzsignments. Begun in 2005 with 41 consigners, her twice-a-year megasale has grown to include more than 150 consigners and a 5,500+-square-foot location. Parents bring their children's outgrown clothes and toys to Laurie and her team, who sell them at the event. Consigners earn 60 to 75 percent of the sold items, are welcome to shop the event yearly for gently used toys and clothes that fit their own current needs, and can feel good about their decision to reduce the need for new products by offering their items and reusing someone else's. For more information about this concept, visit www.kidzsignments.com.

Reusing products is one of the best ways to reduce our environmental impact. As you and your family become better reusers, challenge your kids to come up with even more ways to make use of the supplies you have on hand. Begin to think of yourselves as treasure hunters and embrace opportunities to find treasures hidden among the once-discarded trash. Instead of handing them a new toy from the store, hand over a brown bag filled with various containers. Instead of thinking that your teens are too old for yard sales, help them run one for their sport's team fund-raiser. Reusing products from yesterday makes for a more eco-friendly today and a greener tomorrow.

Chapter Checklist

☐ We will begin to see multiple potentials for all products we have on hand.

☐ We can focus on one "disposable" item we frequently purchase and turn it into something new.

☐ We will look for age-appropriate opportunities to help our family reduce.

☐ We can follow the lead of other environmentally minded organizers and look to bring those ideas into our community.

☐ We will remember that new is not necessarily better for our family or the environment, and we will make a commitment to lead by example.

Recycle: Turn It Around

After rethinking, reducing, reusing, refilling, repairing, rearranging, refurbishing, and reinventing what we have on hand to make the most of each and every purchase, we can talk about recycling. Recycling is the last of the 3R's, our last chance to salvage a product's resources. While recycling is good for the environment, reducing and reusing are ideal. So before you head out to the curb to leave recyclables for pick-up, give everything you're turning over a last look. Once you're satisfied it's time to recycle, your products will enter a three-part circular loop in their journey to become post-consumer items.

First, recyclables collected curbside and at drop-off locations are taken to a recovery center where they are sorted. After they're cleaned and separated, they can be manufactured into new products that feature total or partial recycled content. Buying recycled products "closes the loop" on production and creates that "cradle-to-cradle" existence we talked about earlier in this book. As an eco-savvy shopper, you'll want to precycle before making any purchases, look for recycled items to buy, and familiarize yourself with advertising jargon to help you make more informed consumer choices.

Five-Minute Makeover

If you want to find out the closest recycling center to your home, or your favorite vacation spot, visit www.earth911.org. Type in what you want to recycle and the zip code of your location, and you'll be told where to go. The site is dedicated to being a leading environmental resource and is loaded with informative articles.

The Power of Precycling

According to the EPA, the average American generates over 4½ pounds of garbage each day. That means, collectively, we create over 230 million tons of trash each year. The Earth Works Group, an environmental group committed to the three R's, has found that a third of all this garbage is packaging. That's an astounding amount of preventable waste, and another area where we can take immediate and efficient steps to change our habits.

Packaging is purposeful. It can protect and contain products for transport and sale, keep items fresh, promote sanitary conditions, and prevent breakage. When used modestly, it does just that. But in the last few years, packaging has taken a turn for the worse. Instead of being designed from a practical point of view, with an emphasis on the least amount of product needed to do the most efficient job, packaging has become a prized advertising scheme. Excessively large packages and shopping bags with bright designs and catchy logos are designed with the consumer, not the environment, in mind. And while you may opt to recycle the product's package when you're finished with it, you may not have considered how many layers of packaging it actually had.

Most consumer goods have three layers of packaging:

1. **Primary packaging**—The actual container that holds the contents of the product you're buying

2. **Secondary packaging**—The boxes, plastics, and cases used to contain and transport primary packages to the consumer

3. **Transit packaging**—The wooden pallets, containers, heavy-duty plastic wrapping, and content foams used to ship the secondary packaging.

In 1995 *Discover* magazine first revealed that about 15 percent of our landfills contain food packaging—that's 30 million tons of trash a year; a problem that continues to grow. Why the excessive packaging? Because we asked for it. We want to enjoy food and beverages from all over the world. To meet our high sanitation standards and prevent spoilage, we need to rely on excessive packaging. Thanks to urban sprawl, we live farther away from our "area" food sources, making packaging necessary. Our busy lifestyles have also increased the demand for prepackaged portion foods, such as on-the-go snack sizes and microwavable meals. Add to this our health-conscious desire to have pre-portioned single-serve meals, complete with nutrition and ingredient facts, and it's easy to see how we've ended up in such a mess.

The EPA broadly defines excessive packaging as "any material that is not absolutely necessary for storing a product, protecting its shelf life, or communicating essential information." So what constitutes absolute necessity and what doesn't? For the eco-friendly consumer who wants to make better packaging choices but still has to get dinner on the table, your family can employ simple strategies to reduce packaging waste.

We know that we all have to eat. And most of us need to eat quickly and conveniently. In Chapter 8, we'll look at different ways to eat more responsibly, but right now, we can make huge strides toward solving our packaging problem in one simple step: buy in bulk. By rethinking your dependence on single-serving containers and making a commitment to portion your servings yourself at home into recyclable containers, you will be doing the environment a huge favor. Here are a dozen common single-serve products that can be traded in favor of more eco-friendly packaging:

- **Drink mixes**—A new phenomena in drink mix packaging is the tiny, 1-quart serving of powder packed into a bigger cylinder. Dump in the powder, add water, and mix. Avoid the extra packaging step by buying a bulk container of powder and measuring out the two or three scoops needed for each use. If you already have these eco-offenders on hand, be sure to reuse the containers as paint or glue cups in your kid's playroom.

- **Yogurt**—Single-serve yogurt containers are often made in non-recyclable plastic (you'll find more information about plastics later in this chapter). Buy a large yogurt container and dish out your servings, and then use the container for storing hair accessories, game pieces, or crayons. If your family favors flavor, try adding frozen organic fruit. Defrost the amount of fruit you need for a single serving, add to yogurt and sweeten with honey if desired. This ensures that you can get fruit-flavored yogurt all year round.

- **Juice**—Juice boxes are a one-time-use purchase that all too often find their way into the garbage. Make your own juice from concentrate in a reusable pitcher or buy a gallon jug that later can become a penny bank. For juice on the go, try a sports bottle from the Sigg line. Made from a single piece of aluminum, these bottles are spill-proof, leak-proof, and 100 percent recyclable. With 144 bottle designs and 22 interchangeable lids, your kids can enjoy personalizing their own sports bottle. Visit www.mysigg.com for a complete selection of kid and adult products.

- **Applesauce**—Here's another problematic plastic used for single-serve snacks. Opt for the glass jar and portion out your servings at home. Rinse the jar and turn it into a summertime keepsake. Create a decorative beach scene by filling it with sand, shells, water, and memories.

- **Cereal**—Mini cereal boxes are a packaging nightmare. The small amount of cereal is usually packed in a bag, in a box, that sits on top of a holding box, which is then covered with shrink wrap. Choose a regular box of cereal instead.

- **Granola bars**—Although these snacks are convenient and a healthier option than cookies and candy, they require packaging to maintain freshness. Try this easy homemade recipe, compliments of my fellow eco-friend Anna Tillinghast, with your kids instead and enjoy a fresh product with no packaging waste.

Tillinghast Trail Treats

¾ cup almond butter (or peanut butter)
¼ cup cashew butter (or peanut butter)
½ tsp. vanilla
⅓ cup honey
½ cup sunflower seeds
⅔ cup chopped walnuts
⅔ cup raisins
⅓ cup chocolate chips
3 cups organic brown rice krisp cereal (or Rice Krispies)

1. Beat nut butter, honey, and vanilla together.
2. Add seeds, nuts, raisins, chips, and mix.
3. Stir in cereal.
4. Press into buttered 8×8 pan and chill in fridge for 2 hours.
5. Cut into squares or roll mixture into little balls before chilling. This is especially fun for toddlers to do, and a great way to include them in the kitchen.

- **Carrots**—I recently saw carrot sticks pre-portioned into several mini plastic bags that were held together by a larger plastic bag. Skip this waste by buying fresh carrots and peeling and slicing as needed.

- **Microwave popcorn**—Here's another package (bag), within a package (cellophane), within a package (box) problem. Enjoy a healthier alternative by popping your own stovetop corn.

- **Microwaveable meals**—These convenient dining options target singles or families who eat at different times. But their excessive packaging and high preservatives make them a less-than-savvy choice. When planning for single-serve menus, try making bigger meals ahead of time and saving leftovers for the following day; preparing an "appetizer" dinner with lighter fare like cheese, fruit, and crackers; or having fast and satisfying breakfast foods like oatmeal, hardboiled eggs, and fruit for dinner.

- **Ice pops**—Homemade ice pops are a great alternative to store-bought treats, offering an easy way to reduce packaging waste while reusing the containers you already have on hand. Fill used yogurt cups and the like with juice and freeze.

- **Cheese snacks**—Choose to slice your own cheese and skip the cheese sticks. Store in airtight, reusable containers for easy travel.

- **Dry goods**—Set your sights beyond the food aisles and begin to look at dry good options when shopping. Purchase bulk shampoos and conditioners, and refill your smaller bottles; skip travel-size items and reuse small containers; and resist impulse buys while checking out. These small, tightly packaged products (like batteries) most likely have more environmentally friendly counterparts that you can purchase in bulk next time.

Once you make these simple changes in your grocery shopping, you'll begin to see packaging from a whole new perspective. This precycling approach is a proactive way to reduce your family's environmental impact. Make your children part of the eco-action by designating them "Waste Watchers." At the store, encourage them to find alternatives to the single-serve products you used to rely on. If no options are available, challenge them to come up with their own ideas. Try this rainy-day activity for your indoor environmentalists: Many people like to carry tissues in their purse, briefcase, or school bag and rely on store-bought mini packages that are self-contained in plastic and sold in larger packs. Using recyclable supplies from around your house and a handful of tissues from the bathroom, have children design an attractive, useful, and reusable carrying case for the cold season.

You might feel overwhelmed by the "break it down" process when you get your bulk items home. Since you're used to unpacking your bags and reaching for whatever you need whenever you want it, you'll want to set yourself up for success by enlisting the help of your family. Once cold items are refrigerated, have your children gather up Tupperware and reusable plastic containers, and set them to work. Since even the youngest in your brood can put a handful of pretzels in a small Tupperware container, put children in charge of their snack items. Designate a shelf for the newly packed goodies so kids can help pack their own lunch. Have children mix drink powders and refrigerate them in pitchers, using leftover juices for ice pops. When the time is right, try a batch of homemade granola bars. Remember, you can't go green on your own. Including your children in this process is a wonderful way to lighten your own burden and help them learn more eco-friendly ways of living.

Lunch on the Go

Your green grocery efforts don't have to end at home, either. Packing a less wasteful lunchbox helps teach young students that environmental efforts can—and should—be made in all aspects of our lives. We recycle at home and at school. We turn off the lights at home and at the office. We reuse our dishes at home, and we should do it at school as well. Experts estimate that disposable school lunch waste is responsible for 67 pounds of waste per child, per school year; that's about 18,000 pounds of waste for an average-size elementary school. Take a step in the green direction by helping your kids combat cafeteria waste. If you're used to packing a disposable lunch, choose one day a week as your Waste-Free Lunch Day and try these ideas:

- Pack an appropriate amount of food, to limit waste
- Bring home leftovers
- Use recyclable containers
- Use cloth napkins
- Bring a thermos
- Use a lunchbox and fill it with snacks pre-portioned at home

According to the U.S. Department of Education, over 20 million students bring their lunch to school every day. Help your students implements these ideas, reduce their waste, and look great doing it with inspired eco-products for lunchtime:

- Invest in the Klean Kanteen, a 100-percent stainless-steel thermos that's dishwasher safe and nontoxic, and holds hot or cold beverages. Available at www.kleankanteen.com.
- Visit www.wrap-n-mat.com for a washable sandwich wrap that opens out to a placemat.

◈   Check out www.laptoplunch.com for a fashionable, eco-friendly lunchbox that is reusable, recyclable, and dishwasher safe. This site also provides healthy lunch ideas.

As you begin to build your new Waste-Free Lunch routine, expand it to more days until you have fully transitioned. Look for ways to troubleshoot common problems with your children. Avoid accidentally throwing out cloth napkins by packing a brightly patterned one. Write your child's name on the bottom of his thermos so it can be returned to him if he leaves it behind. Choose an easily collapsible cloth bag as a lunch sack if your daughter must rush to another class directly from the cafeteria. Making changes in dining habits will take time and there may be a few setbacks along the way, but looking for ways to make a no-waste lunch happen is well worth the effort.

These lunchtime ideas can easily translate from the school room to the board room. Packing your own lunch is a cost-effective, healthy, environmentally responsible alternative to ordering in every day. Here are some ideas for eco-eating at the office:

◈   **Ask for assistance**—Why should Mom or Dad have the responsibility of packing everyone's lunch? Teach responsible eating habits by empowering your kids to pack their school lunches—and your office lunch as well.

◈   **Have no-waste breaks**—Bring a mug to work for coffee breaks, and skip the Styrofoam.

◈   **Take-out emergencies**—When you must take out, take only what you need. Ten ketchup packets aren't necessary when you need only two.

◈   **Use, or request, a refrigerator for the office so your co-workers can join your eco-efforts**—Keep bulk condiments on hand for takeout days, and provide an easy space for take-from-home lunches.

◈   **Cut out the paper plates**—Donate old dishware to the office to eliminate paper product waste.

◈   **Water tips**—Keep a pitcher of cold water in the fridge, put a filter on the kitchen's tap, or ask about getting water delivery, to cut back on plastic bottles.

Buying Recycled

In an effort to help consumers make the most environmentally sound purchases, the Federal Trade Commission and the Environmental Protection Agency have developed guidelines to help ensure that eco-marketing is clear and effective. Three major components of this effort are the designation of recycled-content products, postconsumer content, and recyclable products.

Recycled-content products are made from what would otherwise have become trash. When your recyclables complete the three-phase journey and become a new product, they can be labeled "recycled." Recyclable items either are reduced to raw materials and used for new products or are rebuilt, remanufactured, or remade by the product's original company. For instance, Company A's plastic bottles could be turned into Company B's floor tiles, or Company C's toner cartridge could become Company C's recycled toner cartridge. Look for specific amounts of recycled content, such as 100 percent recycled paper, and be wary of vague claims like "now more recycled content."

Postconsumer content refers to materials that were actually used by private consumers or businesses and should be clearly stated. If a product is labeled "recycled content," it could contain both postconsumer waste and various reused product materials, like resources that were damaged at the manufacturing site and included in reproduction. "Preconsumer content" refers to any scraps or excess materials that are "recycled" internally. For example, a carpet company that collects all of its own remnants and fashions welcome mats out of these scraps could claim "preconsumer recycled content." In essence, this means the production line is cleaning up after itself.

Recyclable products can be recycled, but they aren't made with recycled material. It's up to the buyer to recycle it after using it. Saying "made with recyclable content" is not the same as "made with recycled content." Although plastic is recyclable, if your curbside pickup doesn't collect #5 plastics, for example, it's up to you to make sure the purchase becomes recycled material. As your family becomes more eco-friendly, label reading will naturally extend beyond the back of the bottle for ingredient listings to the bottom of the bottle for recycling ingredients. The more you know, the greener your decisions can be.

Recycling: Know Your Plastics

Plastic containers have become such an integral part of our routine that we hardly even notice we're using them. From packaging to toys to picnic tables, plastics are everywhere. When we talk about recycling plastics, we almost immediately think clear plastics, like water bottles. And although I want to focus on the damage these drinks are doing to our Earth, it's important to appreciate that plastic comes in all shapes and sizes, each playing its part in our eco-movement.

The benefits of recycling plastic are a numbers game, literally. As you learned in Chapter 3, you'll find a number on the bottom of almost all plastic containers. Most likely, it will be surrounded by an easily recognizable recycling symbol, often called "three chasing arrows," which form a triangle. Knowing what each of these numbers represents is an important step in precycling and a necessary step in recycling.

Type of plastic: Polyethylene terephthalate (PETE or PET).

Common container uses: Most single-serve water bottles, soft drink bottles and cans, peanut butter jars, and oven-ready meal trays.

Can become: Beverage and food containers, luggage, film.

Type of plastic: High-density polyethylene (HDPE).

Common container uses: Detergent bottles, grocery bags.

Can become: Recycling bins, motor oil bottles, buckets.

Type of plastic: Polyvinyl chloride (PVC).

Common container uses: Window cleaner bottles, cling film, window frames, carpet backing, floor tiles, food trays.

Can become: Traffic cones, garden hoses, loose-leaf binders.

Type of plastic: Low-density polyethylene, commonly called LDPE.

Common container uses: Grocery store bags, most plastic wraps, frozen food bags.

Can become: Compost bins, trash cans, floor tile.

Type of plastic: Polypropylene (PP).

Common container uses: Some baby bottles, most Rubbermaid products, microwave meal trays, medicine bottles, yogurt cups.

Can become: Ice scrapers, bike racks, rakes.

Type of plastic: Polystyrene (PS).

Common container uses: Takeout containers, plastic cutlery, protective packaging for electronics (like CD covers).

Can become: Egg cartons, foam packing, thermal insulation.

Type of plastic: Other—catchall for polycarbonate materials and miscellaneous materials.

Common container uses: Most baby bottles, "sippy" cups, plastic plates, reusable water bottles.

Can become: Bottles.

Five-Minute Makeover

If your family loves yogurt but you're discouraged by its harder-to-recycle #5 packaging, you may be interested in Stonyfield Farm's commitment to reusing. Knowing that polypropylene #5 plastic packaging is a challenge to recycle in many areas, the company welcomes you to mail your cleaned containers back to them. Send them to: Stonyfield Farm, 10 Burton Drive, Londonderry, NH 03053. Stonyfield Farm has partnered with Recycline, a company that manufactures personal-care products like toothbrushes and razors using 100 percent recycled material for plastic handles. Your returned containers will be recycled into new materials and not end up in a landfill. For more information about this innovative project and to shop its online store, visit www.recycline.com.

Whenever possible, check the numbers and precycle accordingly. Most curbside recycling programs accept #1 and #2, with #5 containers being the least likely to be accepted. Plastics #1, #2, and #4 are considered safer, as they require fewer toxic additives to be manufactured; #3, #6, and #7 are made with more hazardous materials. Plastics should never be used in the microwave or dishwasher; high temperatures and prolonged exposure to moisture may be linked to deterioration, causing harmful toxins to leach into food. Opt for plastics that say "no phthalates" or "no bisphenol," heat microwavable foods in ceramic dishes covered with wax paper, and wash plastics in warm, soapy water.

If trying to sort through plastic facts and figures seems arduous, keep things simple by simply avoiding plastic when you can. Pack your own lunch instead of relying on takeout; prepare simple, fresh meals instead of prepackaged frozen dinners (there are suggestions in Chapter 8); and scour secondhand stores for cloth and wooden children toys. It's probably not possible to eliminate all plastic containers from your life, but knowing the facts can help you make more eco-friendly decisions.

Problematic Plastics

Unfortunately, just because something can be recycled doesn't mean it will be. According to environmental groups, plastic waste is increasing, but plastic recycling rates are down. While curbside pickup or recycling drop-off plants have become the norm for almost all areas throughout the United States and Canada, many people use and discard plastics when they're away from home, where they're unlikely to recycle. If you stopped at the local deli for a bottle of water, a cup of soup, and a salad, you'd be walking out the door with three recyclable containers, plus plastic cutlery and paper napkins. Whether you ate in the car, outdoors, or at your desk, chances are that when you were finished, you'd be more concerned about not littering (good) and less focused on finding a recycling receptacle (bad). According to *Consumer Reports*, the amount of plastic waste in landfills increased over 11 percent from 1960 to 2003, with plastic bottle recycling dropping by about a third over the last decade.

The American Plastics Council says we could be doing a lot more. As a nation, we are tapping into only 25 percent of our potential recycling ability. With most plastics being made from fossil fuels, a precious resource, it's crucial that we stop treating plastic as a single-use, disposable item. One of the worst culprits? Single-serve water bottles. The Container Recycling Institute estimates that 8 out of 10 water bottles will end up in landfills; that's over 22 billion bottles. Since plastic is not biodegradable, these bulky bottles will be a problem forever, eventually breaking down into smaller and smaller toxic pieces that pollute our land and water. Environmental watch groups like the Sierra Club, National Geographic's Green Guide, and *Mothering* magazine all caution against our increased dependence on plastic bottles.

Five-Minute Makeovers

Refill not Landfill (www.refillnotlandfill.com) is an online campaign to reduce disposable water bottle waste. According to site estimates, if everyone in New York City used a reusable water bottle for one week, for one month, or for one year, it would make a significant difference in reducing waste: in a week, 24 million bottles saved; in a month, 112 million bottles saved; and in a year, 1.328 billion bottles saved. This site encourages you to make a pledge to use a reusable water bottle and post your comments. You can also link to its sister site, www.filterforgood.com, and read additional facts about the small change/big difference drinking tap water can make.

To make plastic bottle matters even worse, reusing bottles may not be a healthy option. Single-serve bottles are usually packaged in plastic #1 and may leach the known carcinogen DEHA under certain circumstances, like excessive heat or moisture. But bacteria has also been found in reused bottles that were insufficiently cleaned between uses, making it a tough call: to clean and reuse or not? If you are assuming that a retail plastic water bottle designed for multiple uses is the answer, consider that the controversial chemical Bisphenol A (BPA) is widely used in #7 polycarbonate plastic and has been linked to hormone disruption and chromosomal damage in lab rats. Since #7 plastic also makes up the majority of baby bottles and "sippy" cups, giving up plastic drinking bottles is a good idea for the whole family.

Here are some ideas that will make this change easier to swallow:

- **Get help for your (bottled water) drinking problem.** Turn to your tap and send packaging companies the message that you will no longer be contributing to the $7 billion dollars Americans spend on bottled water yearly. According to the EPA, over 90 percent of water systems meet their standards for safe tap water. Check for your community's water report and read information about testing your own water at www.epa.gov/safewater.com.

- **If you own #7 reusable plastic bottles, wash them by hand and look for signs of deterioration, like cloudy water when you rinse.** When it's time to replace your bottle, opt for a healthier alternative like Klean Kanteen or Sigg. You can find a wide selection for adults and kids at www.reusablebags.com.

- **Replace your baby bottles.** When baby needs a bottle, choose to give her feedings using plastic bag inserts, which are made with safer #4 polyethylene, or visit www.thinkbabybottles.com for bottles made without potentially leaching plastics or lead.

Invest in high-quality, Earth-friendly beverage bottles that are better for your family's health and safer for the environment. Taking a reusable bottle to school, office, or the park is one of the easiest earth-friendly activities your family can do; and one of the most beneficial.

E-Waste Recycling

With our advances in computer technology comes the need for advancements in recycling technology. While the family computer was once *the* computer, it's far more likely today that each parent and child will have a personal computer, as well as individual cell phones, iPods, and printers. With new and improved upgrades available almost as soon as you unwrap your last techno-purchase, it's important to know where to send your e-waste.

More manufacturers and retailers are offering easy ways to recycle electronics. Since recycling is profit driven, big businesses appreciate that the easier they make their recycling systems, the more likely you will be to use them. Consumers unload unwanted merchandise, manufacturers save money on reusing parts, and the environment saves natural resources, making it a winning situation all around.

E-Cycling Central (www.eiea.com) is an excellent source, putting eco-minded consumers throughout the nation in contact with electronic donation programs across the country. If you can't recycle directly through the manufacturing company, check your options here. The links page has a series of suggested questions to ask potential recycling centers, ranging from identity theft security to incineration percentages, which makes this a smart site to visit regardless of your electronics recycling plan.

Circuit City (www.cc.eztradein.com), Hewlett-Packard (www.hp.com/united-states/tradein), and Apple (www.apple.com/environment) all offer online trade-in options for working electronics like desktops, camcorders, and game systems. Detailed conditions and instructions vary according to company, so visit each site and take comparison shopping to a greener level.

Whole Foods Market is happy to recycle your obsolete one-time-use batteries. Simply bring your items to customer service. For store locations, visit www.wholefoodsmarket.com.

Verizon Wireless stores collect cell phones and equipment from any service provider and recycle or refurbish the products for their HopeLine project, a program that gives victims of domestic abuse free wireless phones and service. Verizon retailers also collect obsolete rechargeable batteries and properly recycle them. For more information, visit www.verizon.com or mail your phones and equipment to Verizon Wireless HopeLine, c/o ReCellular Inc., 2555 Bishop Circle W., Dexter, MI 48130.

Ink cartridge recycling has become so easy, yet over 75 percent of these cartridges end up in landfills. Many printer ink companies attach a self-paid envelope to return your empty cartridge. If you've lost your envelope, visit a PetSmart store and pick up a preaddressed, postage-paid envelope. Drop it in the mail, and PetSmart Charities will receive a financial donation. It's a great way for pet-loving environmentalists to help in multiple ways.

The EPA has determined that televisions contain enough harmful material to ban them from landfills. If you're looking to get rid of yours, contact Goodwill (www.goodwill.org) to see if they can use it. If you're upgrading models, Best Buy will take away your old television when they deliver your new one (fees may apply). Visit http://communications.bestbuy.com. In addition, many municipalities have begun designating specific sanitation pick-up days or a yearly pick-up event for electronics. Check with your local sanitation company to see if they offer this service.

Five-Minute Makeover

Teens feel right at home on the computer. Help them make their whole home a little greener by finding the family information about recycling locations, charitable donations, and eco-minded businesses. They can bookmark sites for you in an eco-folder so when you need the information, it's at your fingertips.

Trash Your Trash Can

With all the good work your family is doing reducing, reusing, and now recycling, you may be wondering when to use your trash can. My best advice is to use it as a last resort. Very few things can't find a home somewhere else, but when conversations turn to recycling, I often hear, "Oh, but you can't recycle that." The truth of the matter is, you probably can; you just need to know where to look. The best place to start is with the product's manufacturer. Let's say your kids outgrow their Nike sneakers. If you were to visit www.nike.com, you would learn that the company accepts any athletic shoes from any manufacturer for its recycling program. Nike uses recycled shoes to build sports surfaces, like playgrounds and basketball courts. You could use the site to locate a local drop-off area or find out how to mail your sneakers (Nike Recycling Center, c/o Reuse-A-Shoe, 26755 SW 95th Avenue, Wilsonville, OR 97070), all in the time it would take to walk over to your garbage can and toss out your old shoes. Rethinking your recycling options can open up a host of other eco-friendly opportunities.

Aside from "traditional" curbside recycling and drop-off centers, there are a host of online opportunities for cleaning out your closets eco-effectively. Online eco-activity walks a fine line between recycling and reusing, but since you're getting rid of the product entirely and have no say over its future use, it feels more like recycling, and that's why I'm talking about it here.

If you want to get to know your neighbors better and do the environment a good turn, check out www.freecycle.org. This non-profit organization puts recyclers in contact with one another. You post what you want to give away (or an item you're looking for) and communicate online with people who want your stuff. This is a great place to get rid of big, bulky things that are expensive to ship, or sentimental items you'd like to see used again.

Taking a few minutes to organize your items and post them online can open up an entirely new recycling outlet for you. eBay has changed the landscape of online shopping and, coincidentally, recycling. You can post virtually anything on this site and make money while doing it. If you've only heard of eBay and are concerned about trying it, check out *The Complete Idiot's Guide to eBay*, by Lissa McGrath and Skip McGrath, and learn how to recycle victoriously.

As with all the ideas in this book, recycling isn't something you have to go at alone. Setting yourself up for success by reducing and reusing with your family means everyone will be better prepared and more willing to recycle. Saving natural resources may not be something your children thank you for yet, but many years from now, their children's children will thank you for a cleaner planet.

Chapter Checklist

☐ We will remember that recycling is the last step of our product's life and will make sure that we've used all its potential.

☐ We will precycle plastics with an eye toward the worst eco-offenders, avoiding those plastics whenever possible.

☐ We will take responsible green packaging ideas into school lunches and the office.

☐ We will stop using single-serve water bottles and invest in a high-quality reusable canteen.

☐ We will be mindful of e-waste and seek to recycle products effectively.

Room-by-Room
Eco-Redesign

I like my house. I like the kitchen pantry, which has plenty of room to organize my food. I like the second-floor laundry room, which makes putting the clothes away much more convenient. And I like my office, where my computer, books, and files are off-limits to my children. But what I *love* about my house are the personal touches that make it an eco-friendly home: the pantry is well stocked with organic products for healthier snacking, harsh chemicals have been replaced by safe and effective cleaning alternatives in the laundry room, and meaningful souvenirs and ideas for future projects adorn my office as a reminder of where I have been and where I am going.

An eco-friendly home is more than a structure where a family keeps its stuff; it's an environment we cultivate. And we want that environment to be as safe, healthy, and beautiful as possible, an atmosphere that is inspired and inspiring. To achieve this, we'll want to make our homes functional, limit our waste (energy or otherwise), look for alternatives to highly toxic products, and create spaces that are warm and welcoming. A healthy home helps nurture a healthy lifestyle.

It isn't necessary to completely remodel your home, immediately upgrade all your appliances to energy-efficient models, or surrender all the comforts and conveniences you've grown accustomed to in an effort to go green. What you can do is focus on the biggest eco-offenders in each room, taking proactive steps to green up your act. In addition to looking at what you want to phase out, you'll want to make some meaningful additions. A home should reflect who you are and what you enjoy. Adding a meditative element to high-traffic areas and beautifying traditionally utilitarian spaces can further transform a house into a home.

Five-Minute Makeover

If you happen to be reading this book on the cusp of a major remodeling plan, consider working with green interior designers. Green Elements Design offers everything from sustainable harvested and reclaimed wood flooring, to paint mixed without harmful chemicals, to recycled content countertops. Classes and consultations are also available at www.greenelementsdesign.com.

Fridge Facts

It's fair to say that kitchens are probably the most popular room in many houses. At once a gathering place, a craft room, a dining area, and an entertainment mecca, kitchens are vital to every home. With so much time and energy being spent in them, there are several opportunities for greening this room, especially when we consider the effect this space has on our pockets and our planet. You may be surprised to learn that the biggest energy offender in your home is most likely one of your favorite—the refrigerator. For two reasons, this appliance is costing you more money than it should and wreaking more environmental havoc than necessary—dust and dials.

Dust on refrigerator coils actually insulates the coil, making the appliance work harder and less efficiently. To deal with the dust, unplug your fridge, pull it away from the wall, and vacuum all the coils. These coils are constantly attracting new dirt and dust, so perform this task once a season to save money and energy. After you've cleaned and repositioned the fridge, place an outdoor thermometer inside it to get the most accurate reading. After 30 minutes, check the reading. The ideal temperatures are 34°F to 36°F for the fridge and 0°F to 3°F for the freezer. These temperatures keep your food in optimal condition without wasting energy.

Five-Minute Makeover

Inside many contemporary refrigerator models is an energy-saving switch that helps the unit run smoothly. If the switch hasn't been turned on, your fridge could be overworking, simultaneously trying to cool its contents while warming its outer walls. Be sure to flip the switch on and end accidental energy waste. Also look for energy-saving settings on your dishwasher, air conditioner, washing machine, and clothes dryer. If such a setting isn't easy to find, check the owner's manual to see if this feature needs to be activated. For instance, when we purchased a digital air-conditioning unit, we were disappointed that there wasn't an energy-saving button, but after reading the manual, we realized that we could follow the digital prompts and set the temperature and running time accordingly.

Today's midline models are twice as efficient as the same-size refrigerators that were popular 30 years ago, with eco-minded brands being designed to keep contents fresher—meaning less wasted food and less energy used, for dual financial savings. When it's time to purchase a new refrigerator, consider the benefits of Energy Star appliances, which can save single-family households up to $70 a year on their electric bill because these appliances are up to 15 percent more efficient than other contemporary models that don't have the same standards. Energy Star's strict guidelines were designed by a joint commitment from the Environmental Protection Agency and the U.S. Department of Energy. All brands are eligible for this designation, but must meet Star criterion such as using 10 to 50 percent less energy than is federally mandated. How big of a difference can an Energy Star product make? The site www.energystar.gov estimates that Americans saved approximately $14 billion on utility bills and avoided greenhouse gas emissions equivalent to those from 25 million cars in 2006 alone. That's an impressive savings, both financially and environmentally.

If your current appliance is 12 to 15 years old, opt for an Energy Star–awarded model with a freezer on top (these models are least likely to need repair). Avoid side-by-side models and automatic ice-makers or water dispensers; these features require additional energy, which can be avoided by using old-fashioned ice trays and a pitcher of water kept cold in the fridge.

What goes on outside your fridge is just as important as what's happening inside. Since family members will take several trips to this appliance each day, make it a beautiful focal point for the room. Many recycling programs insist that you remove the caps from water bottles or sports drinks before setting out the recycling can. You can reuse the discarded tops as homemade magnets with the following kid-friendly activity.

Pretty Pop Tops

Supplies:
Magnetic strip, available at craft stores
Bottle caps
Scissors
Hot glue gun
Elmer's glue bottle
Paintbrush
Small decorative items: shells, pebbles, beads, and more

Directions:

1. Brush inside of bottle caps with glue.
2. Place decorative items inside, filling the space, and let dry.
3. Brush glue around the outer rim of the cap and continue embellishing with decorative pieces. Let dry.
4. Have older children (or a parent) cut a magnetic strip to fit across the "top" of bottle cap, and hot glue in place.
5. Let dry completely.

Use a single cap to hang light memos on the fridge, or hot glue several completed caps together for larger projects.

Since the refrigerator tends to be the place where important memos pile up, elect a child as "Magnet Monitor." Once a week, the child should take everything off the fridge, wipe it down, and weed through the paperwork. On our fridge, each person has a heavy-duty magnet with his or her own initial. Doctor's appointment cards, phone messages, and to-do lists are organized each weekend; obsolete paper is recycled.

A neat and tidy refrigerator door is more pleasant to look at and helps set the stage for your entire kitchen.

Family Room Fun

If the walls in your family room could talk, they just might tattle on the trouble your carpeting can cause!

Family rooms are a retreat from the hustle and bustle of our public lives, where we can truly kick up our feet and relax. But thinking about the indoor air pollution in your TV room could make for some restless nights. Carpeting makes rooms feel warm and cozy, exactly what we want, but the dangerous chemicals used in its manufacture and installation are worth further investigation, especially when we consider that carpeted rooms are favored by children for playing.

Wall-to-wall carpeting involves more then just the layer we see. It includes the whole system necessary to keep it in place and raise its retail value: backing, underlay, glues and adhesives, stain repellant, and flame-retardant. The chemicals used in these last two processes have been linked to problems ranging from asthma to migraines. Synthetic carpeting, which uses nylon or polyester fibers, contains VOCs (volatile organic chemicals), the same carcinogens that are found in pesticides. Walking and playing on carpeting "kicks up" the chemicals, which are then breathed in; they don't just evaporate.

The ideal solution is to remove wall-to-wall carpeting and opt for hardwood floors whenever possible. To create comfortable play spaces, choose area rugs that can be picked up so the floor underneath and the carpet itself can be sufficiently cleaned. If this isn't an option in your home, invest in a high-quality HEPA vacuum cleaner that's well sealed to help suck up and remove chemicals, dirt, and dust. These high-efficiency particulate air filters are specially designed to absorb the most microscopic allergen, an important consideration if you have children or if anyone in your family suffers from respiratory issues. Experts don't recommend steam-cleaning wall-to-wall carpeting; damp carpeting can become a haven for mold, mildew, or dust mites.

If wall-to-wall carpet is a must-have on your interior design to-do list, consider the benefits of investing in natural wool carpeting that isn't contaminated with chemicals. Visit www.ecobydesign.com or www.naturalhomeproducts.com, and check out carpeting options that will have everyone in your family breathing easier.

Five-Minute Makeover

If you like the idea of deodorizing your carpet before vacuuming it, skip the commercial products and sprinkle baking soda around the room instead. Many commercial carpet products contain chemical fragrances that merely mask odor and aggravate upper respiratory problems. Neutralize odors safely with baking soda; then vacuum the floor 15 minutes later.

Regardless of whether you have wall-to-wall carpeting or area rugs, help stop dirt in its tracks by insisting that everyone remove shoes while indoors. Place doormats outside all your home's entrances, and make it a family rule that all family members wipe their feet before stepping out of their shoes. When weather permits, keep the windows open and cool off with ceiling fans instead of air conditioners, giving carpeted rooms the benefit of ventilation. If children favor your carpeted rooms, help keep play areas better protected by making these Colorful Covers to play on.

Colorful Covers

Supplies:
Old bed sheet (light colors work best)
Assorted food coloring
Vinegar
Water
Spray bottles or water guns

Directions:
1. Hang an old bed sheet outside with clothespins, or drape it over a fence.
2. Mix 1 cup water, 1 teaspoon vinegar, and several drops of food coloring in a dish, making as many variations of colors as you want.
3. Fill spray bottles or water guns with solution.
4. Spray sheet with solution, making a colorful and unique design.
5. Let dry in the sun.

Roll your Colorful Cover over the carpeting and play.

Wash the cover weekly.

Over time, the food-coloring designs will fade if the sheet is made with cotton. But since this project makes good use of food coloring, chemicals better suited for crafts than digestion, and reuses discarded sheets, I think it's worth it. When the cover has run its course, cut it in strips and use it for rags. Then make a new one!

Most interior designers would likely recommend sticking with coordinating patterns, but adding a child-inspired bit of whimsy to your family room won't just brighten the room—it will lighten your spirit. Beautiful in the way only homemade crafts can be, this cover is also useful against dust and dirt, making it the perfect eco-addition to your home.

Bathrooms—Water Wisdom

It's easy to take water for granted when we're so used to having clean hot or cold water at our fingertips. We use water throughout our day in so many different ways that making changes in daily water habits can make an enormous difference in our environmental impact. Looking at our water-using habits in the bathroom affords us a great opportunity to implement water conservation routines. In fact, if you're looking for some fast and rewarding ways to kick off your eco-redesign, I suggest starting with water conservation. The ideas are simple and effective, but the eco-rewards are tremendous.

Putting new, simple systems in place helps to ensure wise water use. Everyone in your family has personal water needs, making these changes a great opportunity to illustrate the importance of a concerted family effort. Each person can—and should—play a part.

Green Hygiene

Trying to get family members to reduce time in the bathroom can seem like an uphill battle, but doing a little behind-the-scenes work can help make the transition to shorter shower times more likely. First, reduce your water heater's temperature to 120°F and wrap it in an insulated blanket to enjoy warm bathing without risking burns or wasting energy. Once in the shower, mark knobs with a waterproof pen or drop of nail polish to limit the "not too hot, not too cold" water waste next time you are ready to step in. Getting the knob "just right" means less wasted energy. Keeping showers to less than five minutes can save 1,000 gallons of water a month. If younger children require a bath, turn the water on, let it run until it is the right temp, and then plug the drain. Then fill to a low predetermined mark (it's a bath, not a pool), adjusting the temperature as needed.

At the bathroom sink, the simplest steps are some of the most effective. Turning off the water while brushing your teeth can save about 4 gallons of water per minute. For a family of four, that could mean a water savings of 200 gallons a week. When shaving, fill the sink with a little water and turn off the running tap, and you could save over 100 gallons of water a week. And of course, teach everyone in the family to tightly turn knobs when they're finished with the water. A leaky faucet can waste over 100 gallons of water a week.

Toilet Trouble

When it comes to toilets, we are literally flushing water down the drain. While this is, of course, a necessity, we can reduce water waste with a simple trick. Have children help you fill a recyclable water jug with sand or pebbles. While kids are flushing the toilet, place the bottle in the tank when the water level is low. Your toilet now needs less water to "fill up" and will still work just as well. While at the tank, put a few drops of food coloring in and ask your child to check the bowl. If the color appears, you have a leak. Fixing this leak can save you over 500 gallons of water a month.

Five-Minute Makeover

Check your showerhead's efficiency by placing a 1 gallon bucket under its stream. If the bucket fills in less than 30 seconds, replace the head with a low-flow model.

These water conserving tips are practical and low maintenance; once you put ideas like low-flow showerheads and toilet tank bricks in place, the work is done, but the ecological benefits continue.

Eco-Beneficial Bedrooms

If you want to sleep easy in your eco-decision making, look no further than your bed. Since we spend about a third of our lives sleeping, shouldn't we make sure we're getting the healthiest rest possible? Mattresses and box springs are purchased to last an average of seven to ten years, so buying the right mattress is an investment. If you're in the market for a new mattress, or if your baby is ready to trade in the crib for a big-boy bed, consider your eco-choices.

Ideally, a mattress made with organic cotton and free from synthetic dyes is your best bet. Many U.S. brands wrap mattresses in wool coverings, natural fire retardants, to pass safety codes without having to apply toxic flame-retardant chemicals. Mattresses stuffed with natural latex are another environmentally friendly bet; rubber

trees are renewable resources. Avoid mattresses stuffed with polyure-
thane foam, which contains formaldehyde. When it's time for new
mattresses, invest your money in quality ones; considering that you
use your bed every single night for six to eight hours, this is money
well spent.

If you're set with your furniture, you can look to greening your
bedding. Conventional sheets, pillows, and pillowcases are most often
made with cotton, the most highly antipesticide-treated crop world-
wide. Add to that the toxic chemicals like formaldehyde used for stain
resistance, bleaching for color consistency, and heavy metals used in
color-dying processes, and it could be hard to sleep soundly.

Buying organic cotton pillowcases and sheets for your bedding
helps reduce the billions of pounds of pesticides used in traditional
cotton manufacturing. Wash your pillowcases once a week and replace
your pillows every year or two; dust mites, bacteria, and allergens get
comfortable in the filling pretty quickly. One of the most common
pillow stuffings is petroleum-based polyester, which relies on a nonrenewable resource. Instead, choose to buy organic cotton, buckwheat-
or wool-filled pillows. Your best bet is to comparison-shop online and
find the most economical deals for these pillow choices. Sites to try
include www.anaturalhome.com and www.underthecanopy.com.

But perhaps the best way to learn as a family the importance of
choosing organic cotton is to do it yourself. Much more economical and a lot more fun than just going to the store, you can buy
organic cotton batting and make your own pillows. Hobbs Heirloom
Organics Batting is the only 100 percent organic craft cotton I've
found and is available through online retailers or by requesting a
special order from your local craft supply store. Visit www.
hobbsbondedfibers.com for more details, or do a Google search to
find retailers, like www.nearseanaturals.com, who carry in it your
area.

Once you order your fill, turn an organic cotton baby blanket
into a pillowcase. Fold the blanket in half and sew closed the two
sides that run parallel to the crease to create a pocket. Turn the blanket inside out, stuff it with the fill, and sew the remaining side closed.
Now you can sleep soundly on a homemade pillow that has reused
an outgrown item. A pillow this size would be excellent for travel

or could make a great holiday gift or keepsake. If you don't have an organic baby blanket on hand, you can purchase organic cotton fabrics in a variety of colors and patterns for a fraction of the price you would pay for a standard pillow. Many larger craft stores are beginning to carry organic fabrics or can special order them for you.

When it's time to wash your bedding (usually once a week), opt to do it in hot water. Yes, it uses more energy than cold water washing, but weigh the pros and cons. Using hot water for your bedding is a proactive step against germs, keeping your family healthier. This could mean fewer trips to the doctor, less medication, and better overall health.

Clean Up Your Laundry Room

You're most likely spending an inordinate amount of time with your washer and dryer, but how well do you really know your machines? Once they're installed, many of us likely throw a load of clothes in the washer, dump in the detergent, pick the warm or hot rinse cycle, and head out to accomplish other tasks. But your laundry room duo has eco-friendly opportunities that are well worth checking out.

Many single-family households keep their water heaters set at the common installation temperature of 140°F. But lowering the temperature to a comfortable 120°F can lower your energy costs close to 5 to 10 percent. Clothes washed in the warm and hot cycle will do just as well with this adjustment, and you'll save energy and money. Even better, wash your clothes in cold water and save up to $100 a year. If you're used to washing in warm and hot water, and worry that the cold cycles won't clean, set your clothes up for success with a few simple measures.

- Pretreat stains with a small drop of detergent.
- Fill the washer with water and detergent first, giving it ample time to suds up, then add your clothes.
- Separate loads into whites and darks/colors, and wash heavy materials together. This will also help extend the life of your clothes, since "delicates" aren't being beaten up by jeans.
- Wait until you have a full load to make the most of the cycle, but don't stuff the machine, which will cut down efficiency.

Several eco-friendly detergents on the market effectively clean without harsh chemicals.

Seventh Generation Natural Laundry Detergent—Free and Clear is vegetable based and contains no phosphates (water-softening agents that damage aquatic life), chlorine, or artificial fragrances. According to the company, by switching from a petroleum based liquid detergent to one that is vegetable based, like Seventh Generation, U.S. homes could save 99,000 barrels of oil; enough to comfortably cool and heat U.S. homes for up to a year. This means that you could help clean up the planet just by cleaning your clothes.

Five-Minute Makeover

If you're looking for a way to use up your commercial laundry detergent but are concerned about the chemicals, try adding baking soda to the load. Use half of the recommended amount of detergent per load and add ½ cup baking soda. You'll be using fewer chemicals per wash while phasing in a more natural cleaning product.

Biokleen Laundry Liquid leaves clothes smelling fresh and clean thanks to the addition of natural grapefruit seed and orange peel extract. Since all the ingredients are natural, your wastewater remains safe and septic-friendly.

Products such as these super-concentrated detergents require a mere capful of liquid per load, meaning that each container will last longer, reducing your plastic waste.

Aside from detergents, numerous cleaning agents whiten, brighten, and remove stains. Making your own cleaners is another alternative to commercial products, and an easy project for children. At one time, my laundry room was unsafe for children, with bottles of bleach, expensive stain-removing agents, and store-bought cleaners lining the shelves. Today my kids can be hands-on in the laundry room because our products are natural and safe for them, but still clean effectively. Enlist the help of your children with these three kid-friendly ideas:

- **Instead of using commercial stain removers, try lemon juice and baking soda.** Make a paste of lemon juice and baking soda, and massage it into the stain; then wash as usual. If an unsightly stain needs extra attention, presoak the garment by filling the sink with cool water and adding a cup of lemon juice and ½ cup baking soda. Wash as usual.

- **Instead of using bleach, try lemons.** Buy a bag of lemons and take that lemon-fresh smell to a whole new level. Place room-temperature lemons on the counter and have the kids roll them under their palms, exerting a fair amount of pressure. This loosens the fruit from the rind, providing more juice for squeezing. Cut the lemons in half, squeeze the juice into a bowl, and pour it into a reusable soda bottle. Keep freshly squeezed juice in the laundry room and use it as an alternative to bleach to whiten clothes. If you tend to rely on bleach a lot, make a bigger batch using two bags of lemons.

Five-Minute Makeover

When you're finished with the lemon rinds, put them down your garbage disposal to naturally clean and disinfect the sink.

- **Instead of using fabric softener, try vinegar and baking soda.** Mix one part distilled white vinegar with one part baking soda for an easy fabric softener that also helps prevent static and lint buildup. When you combine vinegar and baking soda, the solution bubbles up, making this a great laundry activity for your budding chemists. This is the "magic potion" we add to the final rinse cycle.

After your clothes are washed, dry them with care. Line-drying your clothing is the most eco-friendly approach and can save you another $100 a year. If you must use your dryer, always remove lint buildup from the previous load first. Choose the moisture-sensor feature instead of relying on timed drying. The moisture sensor will automatically shut off when clothes reach a specific dryness.

This option prevents overdrying energy waste and reduces clothing shrinkage, lengthening the life of your garments. Most companion washer/dryer models can handle the same load weight. If you've properly presorted for the washer, you won't have to worry about "frying" your delicates while your jeans continue to demand heat. If clothes come out wrinkled, skip the commercial wrinkle releaser and spray with a solution of one part vinegar to three parts water, smooth with your hands, and let hang. You'll drastically cut down on ironing. When you do need the help of heat, spray clothes with homemade starch by making a solution of equal parts cornstarch and water. Iron as usual.

Five-Minute Makeover

When it's time to replace your washer and dryer, investigate your options by reading the comparable information found on the bright yellow EnergyGuide stickers required by the Federal Trade Commission. This guide allows you to compare different models' efficiency and projected cost of use over a year so you can make an environmentally and financially sound purchase.

Since I spend so much time in the laundry room, I wanted it to have a little "personality." To make that happen, our family held a picture-making party. Using photos that had been sitting in a box, we cut and pasted a collage that showcased a few of our favorite things: my husband washing his motorcycle, my infant son teething on his stuffed animal, my 2½-year-old building a block tower. None of these photos are spectacular—the lighting is poor or the subject matter off center—but since we could cut and paste as needed, we were able to turn mediocre shots into a superb wall hanging. Now when we do laundry, we have a memory board to look at that reminds us of the people the room helps take care of.

Green Your Garage

We all like to get into a warm car in the morning before heading to school or work, but how you warm up your car can dramatically affect your health. If you keep your car in a garage, it's very important to open the garage door before turning it on. When you start up a cold car, an enormous amount of carbon monoxide is made in warming the engine. Keeping that toxin contained in closed quarters is a hazard to your health. If you have an attached garage and keep the door closed, the danger is compounded. After you pull out of the garage, the fumes are still left behind, and they can find their way into your home through leaks in the foundation or under the door. Protect your family from carbon monoxide by warming your car in a well-ventilated place.

In the winter, we often pull our cars out of the garage so the children will have room inside to ride their tricycles and bounce balls. This has provided some much needed relief from the indoors without their having to freeze in the cold wind outside. But before we head out to our seasonal playroom, we make sure to give the garage a good yearly once-over to make it more eco-friendly. This means checking the shelves and the floors for potential danger.

Keeping chemicals in your garage is a common household practice, but motor oils, pesticides, and cleaning agents can be deadly if children find them and can be toxic to the environment if disposed of improperly. First, weed out what you don't need. Then take proper caution—health-wise and environment-wise—with the chemicals you must keep on hand. Check expiration dates, organize the products you have, and dispose of unwanted or "mystery" containers properly. Never mix chemicals or guess what an unmarked container could be. Contact your local recycling plant for instructions on properly disposing of hazardous materials.

Once you've minimized the toxins in your garage and made it more kid-friendly, help your children better organize their outdoor sports equipment. Designate an area for sand toys, balls, bicycles, and seasonal sports equipment. Hunt around the house for unused baskets, boxes, and hooks, and work with your kids to design a space-saving section where games and gear can be kept. An aesthetically appealing garage makes toys and games easier to enjoy, promoting outdoor fun and creating a sense of ownership. Lessons learned about taking care of simple sand shovels will transfer to taking care of more expensive tools, like gardening supplies. The better we take care of our things, the less we waste.

If grease has stained your garage floor, take steps to manage the mess. Grease stains are not only unsightly, they're slippery. Make your floors safer by removing stains with kitty litter. Cover the wet spot in the evening and sweep it up in the morning. If the stain has set, cover it with white vinegar and let it sit for at least an hour. Cover the vinegar with cornmeal until a paste forms and then scrub vigorously. Sweep up the area. If residue remains, cover it with kitty litter for 24 hours and sweep again.

Talk about safe handling of chemicals with your children to help prevent curious hands from mishandling dangerous containers. A high shelf out of reach may look inviting to a climber, so it's better to lock up the chemicals, explaining in simple terms that this helps keep everyone safer. Locks are helpful while you work toward limiting the need for such off-limit agents by looking for natural replacements.

Your Big Backyard

Creating a yard you can enjoy does more than outline your living space, it increases it. Whether you look forward to pruning an entire wildflower garden or enjoy doting on your balcony's window box, getting your family outdoors and engaged in nature is a wonderful way to enjoy hands-on environmentalism. Since summer is one of the most popular times to play outdoors, take steps to protect your family from unwanted seasonal setbacks; namely, bites and burns.

Five-Minute Makeover

Headed out in a hurry? Essential oils have long been used to repel insects. Wet a cotton ball with vanilla extract and apply to pulse points, the way you would perfume. You'll smell delicious, but no bugs will want to take a bite.

Peppermint's Summer Solution

Sunburn and insect bites are all too often the hallmark of the summer season. Be prepared for these summer setbacks with a peppermint antidote. Place one or two long peppermint branches in a resealable container, like a single-serve water bottle. Pour olive oil into the water bottle, completely covering the branch. Pack the bottle with your beach gear or park lunch, to have on hand for bites and burns. When needed, apply the oil with a cotton swab to soothe sunburn and bites with its cooling effect. Since the leaves remain on the branch, the potency of the peppermint will last longer, making it possible to carry around. If you're lucky enough to make it through the summer with no bite or burns, use the oil to massage sandal-weary feet.

Ground Maintenance

My older son enjoys few things more than playing in the water. Left to his own devices, he would use the garden hose to clean everything from his tricycle to our cars and the neighbor's dog. Unfortunately, a tremendous amount of water would end up being wasted. As much as I love a clean car, I know that using almost 40 gallons of water at the neighborhood carwash or, worse, letting our garden hose take care of our car's dirty work isn't an environmentally sound thing to do. Luckily, with a few well-placed water systems, you can look good in the car you drive and feel good about how it got that way.

Rainwater collection, often referred to as rain harvesting, has been practiced for thousands of years. Today collecting rainwater is an easy way to take advantage of nature's generosity. Filtration systems and water certifications exist if you want to harvest and drink rainwater, but for my family's purposes, we rely on common household supplies and use this water to garden and clean.

One of the simplest ways to catch rainwater is to place a container under your gutter. If you want to collect only a small amount of water, you can slide a shallow pan or pot under the gutter and then transfer the water to a taller watering can later. Just be sure that the container was made to hold water, or you could end up warping its shape. If you want to capture more rain, you will want to remove the last few pieces of gutter piping and place a larger barrel underneath it. A good-size collection container can range from a 3-liter, family-size thermos you would take to the beach, to a 50-gallon sports barrel you would use for a team practice. Once the water is collected, you can either take it from the top or use the dispensing nozzle at the bottom. Before you set the container out in the rain, remove the top and cover the opening with a mesh screen to prevent small animals from accidentally drowning in it. When the rain stops, cover the container to prevent mosquitoes from gathering and use the water as soon as possible.

What's the most eco-friendly and kid-approved way to clean your cars and play with your water toys? Head out in the rain. We live in the Northeast, where there is considerable rain in the fall and spring. When rain clouds loom large, we get out our rain gear, pull cars and toys out of the garage, and take advantage of Mother Nature's car-wash. Rain doesn't make you sick; it isn't something to recoil against. Unfortunately, many people have become alarmists when it comes to any inclement weather. Dressed in rain boots, jackets, and hats, my family splashes, plays, and cleans the afternoon away. Afterward, we head inside and warm up with hot tea and cozy blankets. The world looks different in every season, in every type of weather. Give yourself and your children a new perspective while completing some energy-efficient chores, by trading in your umbrellas for outdoor time.

Serene Spaces

One of the most common ailments facing families today is stress. While a stressful day used to refer to a tough time at the office, more children are showing signs of stress and anxiety, succumbing to the pressures of intensely scheduled routines that range from hours of nightly homework to demanding sports team schedules. Parents who stay at home aren't off the hook, either. Running a household means facilitating everyone else's schedule while cooking, cleaning, and shopping.

All of this running around usually leaves us running on empty, compromising our immune systems and making us much more prone to illness, or whipping us into such a state of agitation that we end up feeling overworked and underappreciated. All of this can lead to insomnia, nervousness, or even depression. Emotional pain can also manifest itself into physical pain, as anyone who has ever carried the weight of the world on his or her shoulders can attest.

Make a commitment to setting up a serene space in your home that feels cozy enough for solitary enjoyment, yet spacious enough for family enjoyment. In our home, the living room's fireplace is a source of comfort. Instead of cluttering this room with a lot of furniture, we have one overstuffed chair, a table, and a good reading lamp. For one person, the space is ideal. But when we all want to wind down, you're likely to find us on the floor in front of the fireplace, relaxing on the pillows we keep stashed under the table for just such occasions. Nearby, a basket of books and some simple building blocks keep low-key activities within reach. No television, no phone, no distractions—this spot is enjoyed by everyone.

I try to spend some time by the fireplace by myself every day. At first, I felt awkward, forcing myself to make a cup of tea and put my feet up for 15 minutes. I have so conditioned myself to multitask that merely having a cup of tea—without reading the paper, writing the grocery list, or folding the laundry—seemed extravagant. I had to remind myself that just about every job in the workforce allots its employees lunch hours and coffee breaks. It was up to me, as CEO of my home, to give myself permission to take a break. Once I did, the benefits revealed themselves immediately. This simple act of relaxation left me feeling rejuvenated and refreshed.

Sitting quietly for a few minutes in the middle of the day helps me remain much more calm and patient with my children as we head toward evening. Instead of feeling like I have no time to come up for air, I've built these few minutes into my routine. On days when I skip my break, I tend to be grouchy and irritable. Taking this proactive, healthy step keeps my spirits in balance and my home environment pleasant. Relaxed and clearheaded, I'm better able to stick with my eco-plans, with the energy to rinse out jars and organize them in our craft closet, or remember to set the table with cloth napkins. I'm also more likely to enjoy the company of my children as they complete their evening eco-activities, with the patience to help them water plants and recycle cans, and have them help prepare healthy meals.

Since these few minutes made such an impact, I looked into beginning a more structured meditation routine. I found that several of my acquaintances had also benefited from downtime. From simple solitude to serious Zen practices, everyone I spoke to and everything I read offered a different way of achieving the same goal. It was up to me to find what worked best for me—and you can do the same thing. Now I set a timer for 15 minutes every morning and sit on the floor, legs crossed, eyes closed, breathing in and out quietly. Giving myself this downtime in the morning helps clear my mind and get me off on the right foot. I encourage you to find your own special place and begin a meditative practice:

- **Choose a time of your day that is free from distraction.** Usually this means early morning or late evening, but during your lunch break or while the children nap can work, too. Having a consistent time will help build a pattern.

- **Find a location that's warm, welcoming, and quiet.** Ideally, this space should always be "ready" for you. Possibilities are a corner of your bedroom, an alcove in a guest bedroom, or a space in the basement where you can have a pillow, a candle, a timer, and a music player.

- **Set the scene.** Begin your meditation by closing the door (if you have one), lighting a candle, dimming the lights, and sitting comfortably on a pillow or mat.

- **Set your timer for 5 to 15 minutes, gradually increasing the time as you see fit.** It helps to have a timer so you can clear your mind without constantly having to think, "How long have I been sitting here?"

- **Consider beginning your meditation with music.** If you think it would be helpful, play a short piece of music or enjoy the prerecorded sounds of crashing waves for about a minute. A CD that fades out after a short period of time can help you transition from your busy day into a quieter frame of mind.

- **Relax.** Breathe slowly and deeply. Enjoy this time and the benefits it brings: a calmer mind and a clearer sense of self.

My young children can't yet sit in meditation, but my family shares a moment of silence and gratitude before meals. Once the table is set, we light a "thank-you candle" (see more about this in

Chapter 2) and each share one thing we're thankful for. Even my two-year-old can participate in this ritual. After we've all shared our thoughts, we sit quietly for a moment before beginning our meal. After dinner, we play quieter games like puzzles and read books. While these aren't silent meditative practices, they do help us to rewind and relax.

Teens and tweens may be intrigued by your new commitment to quiet and opt to join you in meditation, or they may think the whole thing is a bit "out there." If that's the case, look for times throughout your day when you can all make an effort to be quieter. Turning off the radio in the car, eating without the television on, and keeping the morning routine quiet with a no-texting-at-the-breakfast-table rule are all steps in a meditative direction. A calm home helps to create a calmer world where we have the time to take care of ourselves, each other, and the planet.

Once you establish a calming sense of peace at home, you'll want to carry it with you throughout the day. One way to help achieve that ideal is to create a visual reminder for yourself. For instance, in my quiet corner by the fireplace I have a coaster designed with Monet's wildflowers. I use this coaster for my daily tea breaks and have placed a small framed picture of this scene in my meditation corner. While out frantically running errands one day, I spotted a sheet of floral scrapbooking stickers at the store and was reminded of my serene spaces at home. I purchased the stickers and affixed one to the dashboard, near my car's clock; another by the kitchen sink; and one on my bathroom mirror. Whenever I spot those friendly reminders of serenity throughout my day, I try to take a few deep breaths, refocus, and quit sweating the small stuff. This technique has helped me move my meditation practice into my daily life, and it can do the same for your children.

Our friend's son relies on smiley face stickers to keep him on track. He found a way to manage his fear of test-taking while studying for midterm exams one evening. When he was in the comfort of his dorm room, the answers came easily and the material seemed manageable; however, he'd start to unravel sitting in the classroom, taking the test. On his bulletin board was a large smiley face bumper sticker that read "Have a Nice Day." Thinking it would be a good luck charm, he carried the bumper sticker in his backpack. Having this item near him during the test reminded him of how calm he had been in his room. He was able to relax and finish his test without the anxiety he had become accustomed to. Call it a good luck charm, a magic rock, or a meditative focal point; the name doesn't matter, but its effect does. Helping your children find an object that can help soothe a tumultuous experience is a much more natural and eco-friendly approach to stress management.

Look for a cozy corner where your children can simply relax. The space should be simple and sparse. Ideally, you can encourage each member of the family to create his or her own space. Since our fireplace gathering area was such a big hit, we carried this idea into our children's rooms. A pop-up tent with pillows, blankets, and books is a favorite hideaway for our older son; our infant son seems particularly relaxed in an antique rocker we keep nestled in the corner of his room. The addition of a serene space is as important to your home as any of our energy-saving steps; if we don't take time to reconnect with ourselves and rejuvenate our spirits, how can we be expected to find the energy to connect with our environment? Being comfortable in our own skin makes us less likely to fall victim to commercialism, falsely believing that we can buy a new product to feel better about ourselves, and gives us the energy and ambition to follow through with our important green plans. Redesigning our homes can truly help redesign our ecological impact.

Chapter Checklist

- ☐ We will take the suggested steps to remedy the impact of our home's biggest eco-offenders.
- ☐ We will familiarize ourselves with alternative green products so that when the time comes, we can eco-upgrade.
- ☐ We will facilitate kid-friendly activities that give our children the opportunity to make the house their home.
- ☐ We will make handmade art projects to reflect our family's personality.
- ☐ We will create a quiet sanctuary for the family to enjoy together and as individuals.

Table Matters: Eating by Example

One of the most personally beneficial ways to live in harmony with Earth is to eat more responsibly. We have become a society that depends on fast food, consumes enormous amounts of sugar and caffeine, and regards extra-large portions as standard fare. With childhood obesity at an all-time high, our bad eating habits are obviously rubbing off on our children. Now is the time to make a positive change in our diet. And that doesn't mean going on a quick-fix diet, but rather learning about the way food works and how we can make the healthiest choices for our bodies and our planet.

Approaching your diet from an eco-friendly perspective has dual benefits. When we eat well, we look and feel good, have more energy during the day, and rest better at night.

The personal payoff is better all-around health. In its simplest terms, eating well means relying on nature's harvest, eating in season, and choosing to fill the majority of our plate with whole foods like grains and vegetables. Eating the way nature intended, with every crop having a season to plant, grow, harvest, and rest is environmentally sound. Following an eco-diet can be an exciting experience for the entire family, with all household members having the opportunity to expand their culinary tastes.

The key to a healthy eco-diet is balance. We want to learn to balance our portions and satisfy our hunger without overindulging. We can learn to shop seasonally, balancing what we want with what's naturally available. We can learn to create an appealing plate, balancing the colors, tastes, and textures to ensure that we eat a variety of vitamin- and mineral-dense foods.

When it comes to the current culture of eating, we're accustomed to getting what we want when we want it. This can mean blackberries in the Northeast in January, or a prime rib meal in six minutes courtesy of our microwaves. But convenience has a price. It takes an enormous amount of fossil fuel to package, ship, and store out-of-season fruit for consumers. A litany of chemicals is used to preserve frozen convenience meals, none of which enhance the product's health benefits. Add to this our dependence on fast food, and you're talking about a culture whose eating habits leave a lot to be desired. As we shift to a more eco-friendly diet, we'll find that incorporating organic selections into our diet, buying food locally, and eating in season not only can drastically change the way we look and feel personally, but also can change the way we look and feel about food in the context of environmental responsibility.

Eating Organic

A healthy diet begins with healthy food. This used to mean filling your plate with fruits and vegetables, lean meats, and whole grains. Today, though, we sometimes need to reconsider what "healthy" really means. A shiny red apple may look appealing, but chances are, it was grown using dangerous pesticides and synthetic fertilizers. No longer can we assume that all fruits and vegetables are the same. Making informed decisions about the food we choose to eat is vitally important to our health. Since we are what we eat, we need to make more of an effort to eat wisely. Choosing organic helps make that happen.

Several benefits come from eating certified organic food. Foods and beverages that receive the coveted United States Department of Agriculture "Certified Organic" seal must meet specific standards that include: crops grown without pesticides, additives, or genetic modifications; livestock treated humanely, with no hormones or antibiotics administered; and foods processed, packaged, and stored separately from nonorganic products. In an effort to keep costs down and production up, conventional agriculture uses fertilizers, pesticides, and hormones that have been linked to health problems in humans. These problems are becoming increasingly prevalent as more of our foods and beverages are being manipulated by chemicals. To make matters worse, conventional farmland is suffering from these artificial additives and our water supply is being contaminated by runoff. Remember, all our actions have eco-consequences; with conventional food, the problems are severe.

Organic food is fresher, more flavorful, and better for Earth. As consumers have learned about the dire effects chemical modifications have on food, there have been some promising changes. Numerous corporate supermarkets now carry a selection of organic goods, with several chains even boasting their own organic lines. Local health food stores have become community staples, offering a wide variety of foods and acting as resources for eco-friendly patrons to learn more about environmental issues. But an obstacle for many consumers is the higher price of many organic products. Fortunately, as you make adjustments in your eco-lifestyle and replace conventional foods with organic choices, you can start greening your diet by replacing the most contaminated foods with better organic options.

When I began researching organic food, I was introduced to a list of produce, notoriously dubbed "The Dirty Dozen," compiled by the Environmental Working Group, a research and advocacy group in Washington, D.C. The organization analyzed data collected by the U.S. Department of Agriculture and the U.S. Food and Drug Administration regarding pesticide use on produce. Shopping organic can cost you twice as much, but you might feel better about "splurging" on these organic produce items when you see that their conventional counterparts have been found to carry the highest levels of pesticides, with harmful residue remaining even after washing.

The "Dirty Dozen" are these:

1. Peaches
2. Apples
3. Sweet bell peppers
4. Celery
5. Nectarines
6. Strawberries

7. Cherries
8. Lettuce
9. Grapes (imported)
10. Pears
11. Spinach
12. Potatoes

This is an important list to copy and post on your refrigerator. Reference the list before you head out to the supermarket, or take a copy of it with you so you have a good place to start going organic. Since several of these fruits are probably favorites for your family, enlist the help of your children when shopping for organic produce. Play a healthy numbers game by having them check the PLU number on all products. *PLU* stands for "price lookup" and is the four-digit number on the sticker stuck to your produce. Organic produce has a 9 in front of these numbers. If you buy a conventionally grown apple, the sticker reads 4321. If you buy an organic apple, it reads 94321. When you check out, the PLU number registers the cost of the particular item, and you are charged accordingly.

First Organic Foods

If you have a baby in your family, making his first foods organic is a great decision. Babies are especially susceptible to dangerous contaminants because of their small size and developing brains. You work hard as a parent to provide the right kind of car seats, check to make sure the bathwater isn't too hot, and never forget to buckle baby into his bouncer—all because you want him to be safe. Feeding your baby organic food is another safety step you can take.

We make our own baby food using the organic produce we regularly purchase. Making baby food is as easy as making your own dinner. When baking sweet potatoes for dinner, I bake a few extra, let them cool, peel them, and then put them in the food processor with a little water. I then pour the potatoes into an ice cube tray and let them freeze. When I need a single serving of baby food, I just pop a food cube out of the tray and heat it on the stove. For an in-depth resource on making your own baby food, introducing new tastes and flavors, and making kid-friendly recipes, I recommend the book *Super Baby Foods* by Ruth Yaron.

If you want to complement your homemade baby food with store-bought jars, or just have a few "back-up" jars on hand for traveling or babysitters, there are several organic baby food lines on the market. We've tried a few different kinds, and Earth's Best is our family's favorite. From single fruits and vegetables to flavorful combinations and toddler snacks, this USDA Organic line is competitively priced and frequently on sale, and has no added preservatives, fillers, sugar, salt, or starches, making it a staple in our pantry.

As our children grow, we want them to continue eating whole foods, fruits, and vegetables, but it can be hard to accomplish this when brightly colored, artificially flavored goodies beckon from the store shelves. We can monitor meals and snacks without much argument when children are babies, but soon enough, toddlers, then tweens and teens, are drawn to sugary snacks. How can we continue to help our kids make healthy choices without denying them any treats? Thankfully, a more satisfying serving of ecologically sound eating is, in most cases, right around the corner.

Neighborhood Health Food Stores

Health food stores have become staples in many communities, offering high-quality food, local produce, alternative cleaning products, and a variety of vitamins and supplements. Depending on the area you live in, you may have a franchised Whole Foods Market in your area, or you may rely, as we do, on a privately owned main street storefront business. Either way, the contents of the store are geared toward helping families make better choices for better health. Unfortunately, many people still view these stores as places only for "health nuts" instead of the warm and welcoming resource they really are. To help dispel this misconception, I spoke with our area's natural food store owner and operator, Michelle St. Andre, who had valuable suggestions for utilizing your area's health food store.

When I began transitioning to healthier eating, I felt intimidated by all the new brands, unfamiliar products, and foreign names I found on the shelves. Michelle and her staff at Nature's Harvest were kind enough to explain the setup of the store, help me find products I was interested in trying, and patiently answer all of my questions. Michelle suggests speaking with the staff the first few times you shop at a natural food store so you can get to know them and they can get to know you. Patrons who come in and want to make changes in their diet but don't know where to start can find the staff especially helpful. Michelle speaks with patrons to find out what their current lifestyle is like and then makes suggestions for transitioning into healthier eating. As I've discussed throughout this book, making small changes leads to big results.

Overall goals for most customers includes eating more whole foods and relying less on prepackaged items, and eliminating hydrogenated oil, trans-fatty acids, and high-fructose corn syrup from the diet. This may sound like a tall order, but it's made much more manageable in small steps. For example, Michelle often directs customers who want to pack healthier school lunches to move away from conventional peanut butter, which has hydrogenated oil, and try an alternative like almond butter, later swapping sugary jelly for sugar-free fruit spreads, and eventually serving the sandwich on sprouted wheat bread. I was so excited about giving my son a better peanut butter and jelly sandwich that I immediately abandoned our usual bread and jelly also, and made a "health food store" sandwich with sugar-free fruit spread and spelt bread. My son had one bite and refused to eat any more! I remembered Michelle's advice (and my own mantra of "Small changes, big results") and tried a new sandwich later in the week, using my usual bread and jelly with almond butter. My son cleaned his plate.

Today we all eat almond butter and fruit spread on spelt bread and love it, but it took time to get there. It's good to keep in mind that a health food store staff member can help you find the right ingredients to make successful transitions that make sense for your lifestyle and that your family will accept.

Starting Points

For families with young children who would like to focus on one aspect of their diet, Michelle recommends avoiding foods that have any added dyes. While many parents already check labels for added sugar, few appreciate the dangers of dyes. Although sugar must be monitored, the body knows how to process it. Dyes, on the other hand, are completely foreign chemicals that our digestive systems can't assimilate; dyes are an assault on our bodies. The four most popular dyes, mostly used to enhance the look of food, are Red 3, Yellow 5, Yellow 6, and Blue 2. They're found in beverages, candy, baked goods, and even pet food, and have been linked to allergies, tumors, and cancer. Eliminating foods with dyes is a small change that will make a huge impact on your family's health, and your kids can help implement this change.

Five-Minute Makeover

Dyes are also a common ingredient in most conventional beauty products. What goes *on* your body is just as important as what goes *in* it. For a healthier alternative, check out Arbonne International, whose skin-care products are formulated without dyes, mineral oils, animal products, or chemical fragrances. To connect with a personal consultant, visit www.andreatriche. myarbonne.com.

Luckily, dyes are listed on your food's ingredient package. Since some of the first words children learn to recognize are colors and numbers, your youngest readers can spearhead a word search for dyes. Send your kids into the cupboard on an Eye Spy Mission. Have them look for any products that have dyes listed in the ingredients and put them to one side. For many families, this will result in a huge pile of food. Since the biggest culprits are probably your snack and dessert foods, which should be eaten sparingly anyway, put these items on a high shelf and enjoy them in moderation. In the meantime, bring your children to the health food store and look for chemical-free alternatives together. If your conventional brand of macaroni and cheese has dyes, replace it with a box of Annie's Organic Macaroni and Cheese. Same great convenience without the dangerous chemicals. Eventually, it would be ideal to make your own version of this dish using whole-grain pasta and local cheeses, but initially, you'll have taken the first step.

Five-Minute Makeover

Thank your health food store personnel by sharing a recipe you made using their products. Just about any conventional recipe you have can be made with healthy alternatives; just ask. Bring your child's favorite cookie recipe to the store and talk with an employee about finding healthy alternatives. Then share your success story, and your new favorite recipe, with the people who helped it happen.

Since local health food stores are smaller and less crowded than supermarkets, getting to know the employees is much more likely. It's also a nice chance to give your children more shopping responsibility. My older son loves Nature's Harvest and gets his own hand basket there to "shop" with. He heads straight for the cereal aisle, grabs his favorite box, and proudly totes it around. Here, we have more of a chance to talk about what we're buying, explore the shelves together, and chat with neighbors while we do.

Community Supported Stores

Another huge advantage to acquainting yourself with your local health food store is the chance to tap into a community of consumers who share your lifestyle choices. Nature's Harvest, for example, has a bulletin board filled with information regarding yoga classes, Girl Scout meetings, housecleaning services, and homeschooling co-ops. You're likely to see shoppers bringing their own bags and reusable egg cartons to the store; overhear conversations about reducing, reusing, and recycling; and meet other families who are on the same journey as you. This sense of community can't be packaged and put on the shelf, but it's there, as real as the produce at the end of the aisle. If you haven't yet tapped into this eco-fountain of information and support, now is the time to do it.

Think Globally, Eat Locally

Community Supported Gardens (CSG) first organized into well-represented farms in the 1960s throughout Germany, Switzerland, and Japan, making their first stateside appearance in the mid-1980s on the East Coast. From their humble beginnings, when two farms sought to grow ecologically responsible food, there are currently more than 1,500 CSGs throughout North America. The dedication of their volunteers, the responsibility of their shareholders, and the variety and vitality of their crops make these farms a great option for eco-friendly families who are looking to support sustainable farming practices and enjoy organic produce.

CSGs rely on neighboring households to financially invest in the farms. Instead of just purchasing food from a farm stand, customers become shareholders in the farm. Shareholders pay a fee at the beginning of each season, and this investment finances the planting and harvesting of crops using organic or biodynamic growing methods, ensuring that Earth is respected through crop rotation, seasonal growing, composting, and the exclusion of harmful pesticides. Members benefit from a wide range of locally grown produce that requires little, if any, packaging. Eating fresh, local food helps ensure that your body receives the optimal amount of vitamins and minerals, which makes for delicious eating without the use of chemicals.

If you live near a CSG, contact the director and inquire about enrollment. Most gardens have a set time in which they sign up families for the coming season, giving the farmers ample time to prepare to meet the community's needs. At Genesis Farm, in Blairstown, New Jersey, families are invited to become summer shareholders in November and have the option of choosing a single share or a family share, depending on the amount of produce their family will need. Vegetarians usually opt for a full share, picking up their vegetables every week, while other families, like mine, do well with a half-share and pick up their portions every other week.

Farm as a Family

When children have access to CSGs and local farm stands, they learn where food actually comes from. Carrots grow in the ground and need to be washed and peeled before we eat them; they don't grow in plastic bags! When you pick up your share from the CSG, you're getting food as close to its original state as possible without actually growing it yourself. Having your children help wash the dirt off vegetables lends itself to talking about how food is grown in the ground and, by extension, why it's so important to take care of the soil it grows in. If there isn't a CSG in your area, you can make a commitment to frequenting neighborhood farm stands. While these farms may not be organic, supporting local growers still gives you access to fresher foods, supports local economy, and drastically reduces the miles your food has to travel. It's estimated that in the supermarket distribution system, food can travel over 1,500 miles from farm to plate. With packaging, shipping, and storage, the conventional model production spends the majority of its energy getting the food to the store instead of growing the food. Since food is the fuel for our family's body, it doesn't make sense to us that the emphasis is on the packaging instead of on the food itself.

Many CSG also have "pick-your-own" areas where families are invited to really get their hands dirty. From blueberry bushes to vine-ripened tomato plants, filling a basket with produce directly from the source is a completely different experience than walking through the supermarket and selecting produce from crates. Again, if a CSG isn't an area option, look for other opportunities to harvest your food from the source. Autumn is a wonderful time to enjoy apple and pumpkin picking. Planning a day trip to an orchard or a pumpkin patch is a fun way to introduce children to farms, especially if you live in the city, where farming is all too often out of sight and out of mind. The colors, taste, and textures of farm-fresh apples and pumpkins are often in sharp contrast to those of your supermarket's selection, giving children the chance to see everything from "baby" produce on the branch and vine to ripened selections ready for picking, to rotten fruits and vegetables that have passed their prime.

After making your selections, use your farm-fresh apples in a favorite recipe. To really drive home the difference between a homemade recipe and a supermarket product, host a taste test with your children. An educational and entertaining evening can be had as you compare homemade and store-bought applesauce. After visiting an orchard, get your kids excited about being in the kitchen with this recipe:

Homemade Applesauce

4 apples
¼ cup brown sugar
1 TB. honey
½ tsp. cinnamon
¾ cup water

1. Wash, peel, and core apples.

2. Cut into chunks and place in stovetop pot.

3. Cover apples with 3/4 cup water and bring to boil.

4. Add sugar and honey, lower heat, and simmer 15 minutes.

5. Remove from heat, transfer into large bowl, and let children mash with potato masher.

6. Stir in cinnamon.

Serves four.

Once your homemade sauce is ready, provide a bowl for each taste-testing family member. Then place equal servings of apple-sauce from the jar in front of the panel. Compare the two servings for aroma, color, texture, and taste; your family will quickly learn that there really is little comparison. Warm homemade applesauce is more fragrant, more colorful, and more satisfying to eat than any of the store-bought brands. Once your family is sold on your stovetop success, have fun editing the recipe by eliminating the sugar (a great idea when baking with applesauce), adding raisins or berries to the mix, and experimenting with other spices like clover and nutmeg.

Before you throw away those apple peels and cores, enjoy the flavor they have to offer by making your own apple juice. Simply place cores and peels in a stovetop pot, add 3 cups of water, and cook on medium heat for 15-20 minutes. Strain and enjoy. If your children are juice drinkers, this homemade version won't be as sweet as they're used to, but its tart, fresh flavor may still win them over. As an alter-native, you can use this homemade juice as a broth and cook whole grains like oatmeal or rice in it, giving a new flavor to a familiar standby.

From orchard to table, children will enjoy this experiment in local produce. Starting with one simple dish, like applesauce, can spark a whole new interest in homemade recipes. Fresh food cooking is not only environmentally friendly, but it can be educational and imaginative. Comparing and contrasting the various flavors different apples yield, measuring, mixing, and following directions are all important math and science skills. Perhaps even more important for the eco-friendly family, is the chance to experiment with food. By giving children the chance to take charge of the kitchen and choose recipes, we're giving them hands-on opportunities to experiment with food. The more interesting food is, the more involved they'll become in what they're eating. This kind of interest can turn your children from picky eaters to eaters who choose to pick an eco-friendly diet. Once your children experience the joy of visiting local farms and orchards, the next natural step may be cultivating your own home garden.

Gardening

Whether your backyard consists of acres of country land or a balcony overlooking downtown, container gardens are a manageable method of growing your own vegetables. If you already have a thriving garden in your backyard, congratulations! Use your experience and expertise to help others in your community learn to grow their own food by volunteering to teach a beginner's gardening class at your local library or by sharing your family's talents with your child's classmates. If your green thumb is a bit lacking, relax; container gardens are a great way for everyone in your family to enjoy gardening at a beginner's level.

One of the most popular vegetables to grow in a container is a tomato plant. Most tomato varieties will grow in containers and can be started from seeds, making them an excellent eco-experiment for children. Mid-March to April is the ideal time to plant tomato seeds, with germinated tomato plants available from nurseries as early as May. Tomato plants thrive in direct sunlight, so choose your indoor location carefully, gather your gardening supplies, and enjoy growing your own food.

Supplies:
One 5-gallon pot, at least 12" deep, with drainage holes at bottom
and a water reservoir
One pair of old nylon stockings
Suggested growing mix: one part potting soil, one part peat moss,
one part compost
Plum tomato plant
Stake
Old bath mat
Organic fertilizer (optional, but very helpful)

Choose a sunlit location in your home (a south-facing window
usually works best) and place the bath mat on the floor. Since children will be responsible for the care of their tomato plant, it's a good
idea to protect your floor or carpet from overwatering or dirt. You
can wash the mat as often as needed.

Cut one leg off a pair of old nylons and stretch it over the pot.
Have someone hold the nylon in place while you begin filling it with
the growing mix. The nylon should expand to hold the bottom layer
of dirt, which will allow excess water to drain out of the holes but
prevent soil from escaping.

Place the stake in the center of the pot. Fill the pot three quarters of the way to the top and add the plum tomato plant. Cover the
plant with the soil mix. The stake should be sticking 10" to 12" out
of the pot. Water the plant.

Consistently water the plant to ensure that the soil is moist, not
saturated or dry. As soon as you see yellow flowers, rejoice! Tomatoes
are on their way. You may also want to add a weekly dose of organic
fertilizer to your plant to give it beneficial nutrients; this is more
important if your growing mix doesn't include compost.

Transport thriving tomato plants to a backyard garden or separate them into more containers to prevent overcrowding. Enjoy
a room full of tomato plants, or give your friends and neighbors
tomato plants and spread your eco-garden and goodwill.

Once you get the hang of successfully growing a tomato plant,
consider expanding your indoor garden the following season with
container combining. Certain plants, like tomatoes, can actually do
better in the company of neighbors. A good companion container

that can take homemade tomato sauce to a whole new level happens
when you cultivate a mini Italian garden. Combine a small tomato
plant from the previous season with basil seedlings, available from
your local nursery. As the tomatoes and basil have similar needs,
simply continue the gardening practices that served you well during
season one. From your potted garden to your pasta pot, ingredients
this fresh deserve a homemade Italian Tomato Sauce that's been per-
fected by a renowned (in our family) chef, my mother-in-law, Kathy
Coronato. Here's her family-famous recipe, affectionately called
"Mom's Red":

Mom's Red

15–20 very ripe plum tomatoes
1 can tomato pureé + 1 can water
6–8 garlic cloves, sliced
½ cup or more chopped fresh parsley
Lots of fresh basil, torn into small pieces
About ½ cup red wine for the cook, and about the same for the sauce
(optional!)

> Break up the plum tomatoes with your hands, or cut them up.
> Happy hands squish tomatoes better, so get the kids to help.
> Put all the ingredients in a pot and cook on low heat for four
> hours, until the sauce is nice and thick. Stir periodically so it
> doesn't burn. If the sauce doesn't thicken, leave the lid partly
> open. If it gets too thick, add a little water. The longer it cooks,
> the better the sauce.

Like any good passed-down recipe, measurements are less
important than taste. When trying new dishes in your home, use the
recipes as a jumping-off point and make them your own. Consider
simmering sauce with cooked sausage if your family loves meat or
garden vegetables for a lighter addition. Have fun with food as you
consider the wise words of Kathy Coronato, "Variety is the spice of
life, and so with red sauce."

Meal/Menu Planning

As your garden begins to grow and you begin thinking about food
differently, menu planning will take on a more personal perspective.
As I began transitioning to a more eco-friendly diet, wanting to rely

more on fresh, whole foods and limit overprocessed and overpackaged products, it became clear to me that planning weekly menus was a critical step in organizing my kitchen to reduce waste, save time and energy, and enjoy healthy meals. Knowing what I was making ahead of time, having the right ingredients on hand, and doing as much "prep" work as I could before actually cooking has helped me make meals that are satisfying season after season.

Making a detailed grocery list and spending one morning a week shopping instead of making several quick trips to the store saves time and energy (mine and the planet's). Thinking about food in terms of weekly needs, not daily meals, has enabled me to better manage my time during the week. With two small children and a husband who consistently works late, preparing daily dinners from scratch isn't realistic. Despite my good intentions, if I haven't planned accordingly and done some prep work for my meals—whether that means chopping vegetables, cooking beans, or baking a quiche—I end up scrambling at the last minute and pulling out all the products I'm trying to avoid. With preplanning, I have the right ingredients on hand, can prep on a weekend morning to set myself up for success, and then have the freedom (and patience) to bring my children into the kitchen to help with one aspect of the meal, instead of trying to do everything with them underfoot. Even your youngest children can help make side dishes or snacks. My two-year-old has helped slice peeled cucumbers for salad using a plastic knife (which we wash and reuse), break uncooked spaghetti in half for boiling, and wash fruit in the sink.

Since my husband is home on weekends and I have an extra set of hands to tend to the children, Saturday morning is a good time for me to shop for food, and Sunday morning is a good time for me to cook. Find the block of time that works best for you—perhaps naptime, weekdays when the kids are in school, or evenings. Look through cookbooks, check out online sites, and gather recipes before making your shopping list. Once you know the main dishes you'll be cooking, invite your children to suggest fruits, vegetables, and side dishes they would like to prepare.

Eat a Rainbow

My son used to be such a picky eater. Then I discovered the beauty of "coloring" his plate. Instead of just having one serving of one vegetable, we use a variety of smaller-size portions to decorate his plate. Since we've opened our "Rainbow Restaurant," there have been much smoother dinner hours. If you'd like to open your own Rainbow Restaurant, begin by writing or drawing the colors of the rainbow on a list for each child, and invite them to pick out produce at the farm or grocery store the next time you go shopping with them. They can fill your basket as they fill in the blanks.

You can spotlight a color each week and try new foods that fit your focus. Eating red could include basics like sliced strawberries on oatmeal or watermelon slices for dessert, or you could try a new homemade recipe. Salsa is great to have on hand to accompany taco night or as a snacking dip to enjoy after school with raw vegetables and blue corn chips. .

Try this mild and mouthwatering salsa with your children:

Mild-Mannered Salsa

2 medium tomatoes diced in food processor
2 medium tomatoes chopped by hand into chunky cubes
¼ cup diced red onion
¼ cup chopped cilantro
½ green pepper, chopped
½ yellow pepper, chopped
Juice from one lime
Salt and pepper to taste

> Combine all ingredients, then refrigerate at least four hours. Stir before serving. Makes about 3 cups of salsa.

How about making a rainbow connection on your dinner plate? When "Green Team Coronato" sits down for dinner, our plates are colorful and inviting. Instead of just white potatoes, we've added steamed carrots to the potato pot and mashed a beautiful orange side dish. Spices like cinnamon and nutmeg have helped add color, as have sliced fruits like purple grapes. We've even garnished our plates with a yellow dandelion from the lawn to complete our picture-perfect palette! Before eating, a quick game of Eye Spy gives us a moment to check our color combination before digging in.

If your kids have a sweet tooth that's souring your healthy standards, put them in charge of doing dessert better. Seven days of the week = seven colors of the rainbow. Challenge the kids to broaden their idea of dessert while trying new, colorful foods. Sliced peaches served warm with raisins are a sweet and satisfying treat that would make a lovely addition to "orange" dessert night.

Be sure to set yourself up for success by designing a list of Rainbow Restaurant Rules. These could range from which dessert of the week each child is responsible for planning, to how many bites of each new color must be eaten each night. Keep the rules light and lively, like a game. The rules are meant to move the game along, not ruin the players' good time. Once your family business is off the ground, enjoy introducing your little chefs to healthier eating.

Weekly Meal Planning

Once you have your weekly groceries, do as much preparation as possible beforehand to avoid the six o'clock scramble to the table. And when you've seen the benefit of weekly dinner planning, you're likely to extend this practice to breakfast and lunch. Nowadays, I pretty much know what I'm serving for lunch next Thursday, give or take the occasional detour. I keep breakfast fast and satisfying with hard-boiled eggs, baked oatmeal, or yogurt, fruit, and granola, and I make dinner with the next day's lunch in mind. For example, a roasted chicken on Sunday becomes Monday lunch's chicken salad and Tuesday evening's chicken soup. Since the side dishes vary— veggies and potatoes on Sunday, apple and veggie chips on Monday, crusty bread and salad on Wednesday—I have yet to get the "chicken again?" complaint. The latter part of the week I leave for vegetarian dishes, appetizer-style eating, and make-ahead quiches or slow cooker cooking.

In addition, I try to always have a veggie quiche, hummus dip, and whole-grain muffins on hand to grab and go. Does this preplanning pay off? Absolutely. Financially, I save about 15 percent each time I shop because I clip coupons and stick to weekly specials that meet my menu needs. Environmentally, I hit the health food store and supermarket once a week, while out and about completing other errands. We're eating better, feeling better, and enjoying our meal preparations more. I encourage you to do the same.

I also suggest giving tweens and teens the responsibility of preparing one meal a week. For chef-savvy kids, this may mean preparing an entire dinner. For young adults whose after-school schedule keeps them out of the house until dinner, preparing a weekend breakfast may work best. The emphasis need not be on gourmet meals, but on healthy dishes served with care and consideration for the environment and home. Setting a table with dishware and preparing a nutritious meal—be it a pasta primavera or oatmeal and fruit—helps keep kids connected to eco-friendly eating habits. As our children grow from passive to active consumers, it continues to be important to give them regular opportunities to prepare and eat healthy foods.

Moving to a Seasonal Diet

Once you notice the benefits of menu planning—financial savings, more personal time, less environmental waste—you'll be ready to take menu planning to the next level with seasonal eating. You can begin to eat seasonally regardless of the time of year. The trick is learning what is in season, when, where you live. As a rule of thumb, you probably shop by price, drawing the conclusion that when containers of strawberries are being sold two for one, they're in season, and when their price is twice as high as gas, they're out of season. But since prices can vary throughout the country depending on where produce is grown, that's only a general guideline. More important, since your children are seeing the same selections week after week and are probably not paying as much attention to price, learning which produce is in season can be a fun family affair.

While each season provides a generous selection of foods, making a comprehensive list too lengthy, knowing the key ingredients for each season can help get your plate pointed in the right direction.

Simple Summer Dishes

In the heat of summer, our bodies crave refreshing, water-dense food that can help cool us off. Blackberries, blueberries, broccoli, corn, cucumber, mushrooms, peaches, tomatoes, watermelon, and zucchini are abundant this time of year, providing families with nutritious, colorful selections to choose from. Since turning on your oven in an air-conditioned house is a waste of energy and resources, outdoor cooking and noncook dinners make the most eco-sense. While BBQ cooking typically conjures up ideas of steaks, burgers, and hotdogs, lighter fare like salmon is a favored catch of the summer season and has less fat and calories than red meat, with the added benefit of omega-3, a much-needed nutrient for our brains. Try brushing vegetables with a variety of homemade marinades and then grilling them, for a new flavor experience. Kids can help mix marinades or make dips for dunking their veggies. If you're short on time, simply have your child wash his hands, put sliced vegetables in a bowl, add ¼ cup of olive oil, and mix to coat. Add salt and pepper to taste, then skewer vegetables for grilling. This is especially fun if there's a variety of veggies to skewer; kids will instinctively look to make patterns and enjoy skewering "tomato, zucchini, mushroom, tomato." Eating outdoors can make the experience even more pleasurable, giving your Rainbow Restaurant a new option.

Stepping outside for dinner doesn't have to mean walking away from your good eco-practices. Instead of relying on disposable paper goods for your alfresco dining, set your table (and yourself) up for success by setting the patio table with your everyday dishes and silverware. Cut down on the back-and-forth hassle by having your sand toys do double duty. Use clean pails to carry out silverware, napkins, and condiments. Stack small plates on a sand sifter and carry outside. Instead of using pricey (and plastic) table decor, dress up your table with a seashell center piece by filling a shallow container with sand and placing seashells on it. Your table will be inviting and eco-friendly, making it a lovely eating experience.

Five-Minute Makeover

If your kids turn up their noses at veggies, creating a colorful table using their sand toys might just be the added incentive they need to try something new. Eating sliced cucumbers is a lot more fun when you're dunking them in a personal seashell dipping "bowl" filled with ranch dressing. Have fun personalizing your patio dining, and you're likely to find a family of eco-eaters enjoying your efforts.

Fall's Bounty

As the temperatures begin to dip in autumn, watery summer foods give way to drier fare like acorn squash, apples, carrots, figs, pears, pumpkins, rhubarb, and sweet potatoes. Nothing signifies the change in seasonal eating for my family like baking. After a summer spent away from the oven, we look forward to measuring, mixing, and making a variety of warm foods. Since the holidays are just around the corner, we try to hold off on baking dessert items and instead opt to make muffins and breads. And the perfect accompaniment to our baked goods is a good soup.

As much as I enjoy baking from scratch, I don't always have the time to do it; therefore, I find it best to stock up on a few boxes of whole-grain or bran muffin mix from our local health food store. I always add on-hand ingredients to the mix to optimize nutrition and make the most of fruits and vegetables that need to be used before they spoil. My son has enjoyed adding chopped carrots, diced pears, leftover sweet potatoes, and diced figs to his muffin mix. We simply follow the directions on the box, add our extra seasonal ingredients, and bake as directed, using the cooking time as a guide. Since our additions tend to make the recipe more "wet," we check the muffins at the suggested time but usually end up needing to leave them in the oven for a few extra minutes. This strategy has given us the best of both worlds: quick and easy home-baked goods that pack a powerful, and tasty, punch.

For lunch, we often enjoy having muffins with a homemade soup. This is one of the best ways I've found to get my son to enjoy a variety of root vegetables. From squash to sweet potatoes, a food processor can quickly turn a variety of vegetables into a meal. Usually, I do all the stovetop cooking and let my son "make the soup" by putting him in charge of the food processor—a loud, whirling kitchen appliance tailor-made to delight toddlers. Older children can assist with peeling and chopping, with teens being able to handle the entire recipe on their own. As a bonus, soups freeze well, making a large batch an efficient way for your teen to fulfill her dinner-making responsibility today and keep something in reserve for the next time it's her turn in the kitchen.

Super Simple Soup

2 lb. root vegetable (pumpkin, squash, or sweet potato, or a combination of the three) cleaned, peeled, and chopped
1 cup diced onion
1 carrot, peeled and chopped
3 cans chicken or vegetable broth
2 TB. olive oil
½ tsp. chopped garlic
¼ tsp. salt, more to taste
2 TB. butter, divided
½ cup light cream
Cinnamon for garnish

> Combine first seven ingredients and 1 TB. butter in a saucepan. Cook on low-medium heat, uncovered, for 35 to 45 minutes, or until the vegetable is fork tender. Transfer to food processor, and add remaining tablespoon of butter and cream. Blend well. Serve with a sprinkle of cinnamon and your homemade muffins.

Five-Minute Makeover

Nuts and seeds are also readily available in autumn, giving your family another energy-boosting snacking option. Try lightly toasting nuts and seeds on a shallow baking pan in a 350°F oven for five minutes to bring out their flavor. Mix nuts and seeds with whole-grain cereal, raisins, dried cranberries, and/or granola, and store in an airtight container. Fill a reusable snack container with this seasonal treat and enjoy!

Warming Winter Meals

Since we emphasized eating "cool" foods in the summer, it makes sense to look for "warm" foods in the winter. In most areas of the country, winter's cooler weather often brings winter colds and flu. Eating foods in season helps boost your immune system, making it an excellent proactive health decision. Eating a hearty meat stew is a great way to warm yourself from the inside out. As with soup recipes, a nice thing about stew recipes is that you can add whatever vegetables you have on hand and season to taste. We like to slow-cook two pounds of cubed organic meat with a variety of potatoes, turnips, carrots, and brussels sprouts, seasoned with salt, pepper, garlic, and onion powder, and two cups of chicken broth in our crock pot for about eight hours. Before we head out to enjoy a snowy day, we can fill the crock pot with our ingredients, turn it on low, and know that a delicious, hassle-free meal will be ready for us when we return home.

I've been especially fond of adding brussels sprouts to stews since I learned they're a winter superfood. They help to detoxify the body and have even been linked to cancer prevention. Since we spend more time indoors during the winter, I like knowing that this simple diet addition can help rid our bodies of harmful indoor pollutants. If you're interested in learning about the power and potency of different seasonal selections, I recommend *Super Foods* by Delia Quigley. Delia is a renowned nutritional counselor, master yoga instructor, author, and speaker whose work includes educating people about the importance of seasonal cleansing, maintaining a whole-foods diet, and treating our bodies with care and compassion. I have personally benefited from her nutritional counseling and find her book to be informative and accessible.

In addition to cabbage, leeks, potatoes, turnips, spinach, and radishes, winter is a good time to enjoy citrus fruits like lemons and oranges, which are loaded with Vitamin C. An easy way to enjoy these fruits is to add them to a pitcher of water you keep cold in your fridge. During the colder months, we tend to drink less water because we sweat less. But you need to remain hydrated all year, and you can get an immune boost by squeezing oranges and lemons into your water pitcher. A few fruit slices make a glass pitcher of water look more inviting and provide just a hint of flavor. While drinking your immune-boosting beverages, family members can use the remaining fruit slices to give winter birds a much-appreciated treat.

Just as we benefit from three daily servings of fruit a day, birds need fruit to retain optimal health, but it can be difficult for them to find it in the winter months. Your children can lend feathered friends a helping hand by making seasonal bird feeders. All the ingredients listed here are beneficial to birds, making this wintertime activity a nice way for children to appreciate that, like humans, animals have dietary needs. Feeding wildlife helps remind family members that they're connected to nature and gives everyone a chance to nurture.

Pinecone Bird Feeders

Fallen pinecones
String
Chunky peanut butter
Spoons
Citrus fruit
Scissors
Sunflower seeds
Plates

Cut fruit slices into very small pieces and set them aside. Pour sunflower seeds onto plates, spread around, and set aside. Tie a length of string around the top of the pinecone long enough to hang it in front of a kitchen window or from a nearby branch. Cover pinecone with peanut butter using the backside of a spoon. Stick fruit bits onto the peanut butter. Roll the pinecone in sunflower seeds, then hang the bird feeder.

If you live in an area without pinecones, you can clean an aluminum soup can, punch two holes through the bottom, string a ribbon through it, and follow the remaining directions. Be sure to clean and recycle the can when you're finished with your bird feeder.

Every part of this craft is eco-friendly. Using fallen pinecones makes good use of a natural resource that you can later toss into the woods, where a thankful squirrel will claim it. Chunky peanut butter provides birds with high-energy peanut pieces, seeds are a staple in a bird's diet, and fruit, as already mentioned, helps maintain health. Keep in mind that birds will come to depend on these feeders as a source of food, so plan on keeping up your pinecone practices throughout the winter.

Satisfying Spring Cooking

Probably the easiest time of year to embark on seasonal eating is during spring. With local farm stands reopening for business, this is a great time to enjoy apricots, avocados, chives, fennel, leafy greens, pineapple, spinach, strawberries, and sugar snap peas, just to name a few. Spring is our favorite time to enjoy fruit. After a winter spent eating heartier fare, we appreciate the light and sweet flavors of berries and melons, and often have salads for dinner. I used to go a bit overboard with my produce purchases and ended up wasting food—a very environmentally unfriendly thing to do. Learning about the care of food has made a big difference in our grocery waste management.

Knowing how to properly store your fruits and vegetables is critical to reducing grocery waste. Throwing out food is a waste of money and resources, something all eco-friendly families will want to avoid. There's so much to learn about the care of food, and several websites listed at the end of the book will give you more detailed information. For starters, though, consider assigning your children an easy and useful strategy to better care for the family's food.

- **Just as you have a fruit bowl on the counter, have a tomato bowl.** Tomatoes shouldn't be refrigerated; that turns them mealy, causing them to lose flavor. Put children in charge of "Tomato Time," making sure that the items in the bowl are used in a timely manner.

- **Care for your lettuce.** Upon returning from the market, have someone wrap unwashed lettuce in recycled paper towels and return it to its plastic bag. Refrigerate.

- **Keep potatoes in a cool, dry place, like a pantry closet.** However, food can be forgotten when it's out of sight there. Assign a child to be your "Closet Keeper" and make sure that pantry potatoes find their way onto your plates.

- **For best flavor and most nutrients, store citrus fruit in the refrigerator and use it within two weeks.** Have your children keep a "citrus calendar," noting when fruit should be used by. If a spoilage date is fast approaching, brainstorm new ways to use fruit. For example, cutting an orange in half and stuffing it inside a chicken before roasting helps keep meat moist. Fresh juice can be squeezed on chicken or used in beverages.

If at the end of a busy week you find yourself with overripe fruit that's threatening to go to waste, don't despair. A fruit smoothie can be an excellent way to use what you have on hand. Plus, these milk-shakes in disguise have the look and taste of a dessert, making them a fast and fun way to enjoy your fruits and vegetables. Smoothies can be made in a variety of ways, and there are no hard-and-fast rules, but here's a recipe equation that's helpful to remember:

2 parts fruit + 1 part dairy + $\frac{1}{2}$ part ice = Smoothie Success

For instance, if you have 2 cups of strawberries, you'll want to add 1 cup of milk and $\frac{1}{2}$ cup of ice to your blender and mix. You can use a variety of fruits, substitute yogurt for milk, or use frozen fruit instead of ice cubes. In addition, you may want to add a teaspoon of wheat germ or flax meal to boost the smoothie's nutritional value. This is a great way for kids to experiment with flavors while learning that a mushy banana isn't gross—it's just good for something else.

Five-Minute Makeover

Once your kids are sold on smoothie snacks, keep some fresh fruit on hand for colder months with the help of your freezer. Freeze sliced bananas, berries, and melon chunks in reusable containers, and whip up a flavorful out-of-season treat using seasonal ingredients!

Eating seasonally requires a shift in our thinking. It's a more responsible way of eating, as we learn to respect Earth's different growing seasons and eat what's naturally available. It's a shift that takes time and energy; many of us are so used to seeing blackberries, lettuce, and carrots all year that we may not even know which season produces which foods. And of course, it's more ecologically sound eating, as seasonal, local eating doesn't require tons of pesticides and fertilizers to make food grow in an "off" time. With a few simple steps, your family can begin to reap the benefits of nature's harvest and enjoy a colorful array of foods, grown with a commitment to Earth's community.

Chapter Checklist

- ☐ We will commit to buying organic produce from the Dirty Dozen list.
- ☐ We will patronize local farmer's markets.
- ☐ We will experiment with new flavors, ingredients, and recipes.
- ☐ We will all take turns preparing healthy snacks or meals.
- ☐ We will freeze seasonal summer fruit for a winter treat that does not compromise our green-eating plans.

Clean Green

If you've been doing most of the cleaning chores in your home because you didn't want your kids near chemicals or thought they couldn't handle the job, you'll be glad to hear that help with housework is on the way. Learning to care for one's home is how we learn to care for our planet. It makes sense that children who are allowed to leave their toys all over the floor have a hard time understanding why litter has to go in the garbage can. It makes sense that kids who neglect their bicycles, misplace CD players, or lose board-game pieces only to have a new one given to them have a hard time understanding why we have to reduce, reuse, and recycle. Chores are a wonderful way to help teach children that certain jobs must be done to take care of a household and our environment. There's only one Earth. We can't go to the store and get another one. Being a part of the world means contributing to the care and maintenance of our local and global home.

To make your household cleaning routines run more smoothly, equip your children with their own cleaning baskets. First, find a basket or container with a handle that makes grab-and-go cleaning easier. Buckets used for trick-or-treating or Easter baskets are sturdy, colorful products that can be recruited for cleaning duty. Remember, our first goal is to reduce the amount of "stuff" we have by reusing our things in new ways. Why buy new containers when you already have plenty in storage? Fill each with a condiment container with the following cleaning staples:

- Baking soda
- Rags
- Saltshaker
- Spray bottle
- Olive oil
- Bottle of vinegar
- Old toothbrush (which a parent has sanitized by soaking it in equal parts water and hydrogen peroxide overnight to kill bacteria)
- Promotional or expired plastic credit card

Five-Minute Makeover

These baskets could make lovely housewarming gifts for friends and family. In addition, you might like to add the recipe for stovetop potpourri in Chapter 3 to freshen the new home, or fresh dried herbs from your garden, with directions for enjoying a cup of tea when chores are finished.

When getting ready to clean, the last thing you want to do as an environmentally friendly family is reach for a roll of paper towels or ruin your good clothes. A much better option is to have a container of cleaning rags ready. Mismatched socks are a great tool; they can slip over little hands to make cleaning mittens. Cutting old sheets into fabric squares makes useful window and mirror rags. Wearing an old oversized sweatshirt as a cleaning smock can keep your newer clothes clean and get you into chore mode. Using a sweatshirt with side pockets or an old man's work shirt with a deep breast pocket makes it possible to stash the valuable things you find along the way.

Usually, we underestimate what chores our children can help with. But young children make little distinction between cleaning and playing. The chance to spray, sprinkle, and scrub is just another means of fun for them. My older son loves his spray bottles and "taking care of his things." Cleaning with him used to take longer—he's been known to "help" a bit too much—but the opportunity to teach him that in our family we take care of what we own is priceless. I assumed that he would know what to do just by watching me. I found out that I had to be very clear about how to complete a project. As a toddler, he has daily jobs that are focused and manageable. In the morning, he hangs his pajamas on a low clothing hook. His stuffed animal and comfort blanket are put at the top of his bed. Everything has a place, and there's a place for everything.

Whether you have toddlers or teens, several cleaning rules can help everyone complete chores efficiently and effectively.

Buckets to Bookshelves

Toddlers are perfectly capable of putting away their books, toys, and stuffed animals in buckets or baskets. You can reuse laundry baskets or decorate discarded shipping boxes for those purposes. Nothing should just be left out on the floor. As children grow, they can learn to put items back on the shelf where they came from. Don't assume that kids know what that means, though.

To effectively teach cleaning, you need to model, manage, and monitor. For instance, when cleaning up a board game, model putting things away by collecting game pieces and the like, placing them in the box neatly, and properly fitting the top cover over the bottom. Then put the game on the game shelf where it belongs, moving other toys, if necessary, to securely balance it. The next time this game is played with, manage the cleanup by doing it together, while reiterating the directions out loud: "Let's be sure to put the game board on the bottom so the box will close all the way." Finally, monitor how your child cleans up alone. If the game is shoved on the shelf with pieces sticking out, it isn't cleaned up. Don't accept lazy efforts. Dessert, TV, or computer time can wait until the cleaning is done right.

If toys are left out, clothes are thrown in the back of the closet, or board games are repeatedly haphazardly put away, this indicates disrespect for belongings. Once systems are in place, do an unannounced sweep of playrooms and bedrooms, and put the disregarded belongings in a clear container. Inform children that these containers are off-limits and the contents must be earned back. This could mean doing extra chores or an out-of-pocket allowance charge.

How does this translate to your eco-friendly efforts? We have taken advantage of Earth's resources. We need to take better care of what we have or we'll find ourselves without limitless access to its resources. Just as we're required to scale back our water usage during a summer drought, which reminds us how precious our water supply is, we can remind children how precious their beloved belongings are by temporarily taking them away.

This system can work for your younger children, too. When our son mistreats his toys by throwing an action figure across the room or hitting his baby brother with a stuffed animal, the object goes in "time-out." It's kept out of reach but remains in sight. To keep things simple, my husband and I need only say, "When you don't take care of your things, you lose them." This is true of toys, food, and the ozone layer. Taking care of stuffed animals will translate into taking care of wild animals. Including your children in household chores is an excellent way to illustrate this transition.

If items remain in the container for an extended amount of time with no effort made to retrieve them, consider them donations. This is a tough but important lesson to learn. Elementary-school children through teens should experience solid consequences for neglecting their belongings. If after a week the same CD is still sitting in the container, give it away, and don't buy another one. Either your teen will save up to replace it, or not. Either way, it's important for her to learn that she can't assume that the things she neglects will always be there. If we don't take care of things today, they could be gone tomorrow.

Making Chores More Manageable

A cleaning checklist is a nice tool for monitoring daily chores and breaking big cleaning jobs into more manageable steps. For young children, an incentive chart complete with stickers can be effective. Preschoolers can benefit from seeing illustrations of daily tasks and keeping track of weekly responsibilities. A simple checklist like this generated on your computer and printed on recycled paper makes it easy to update and monitor activities. A check in the box indicates that the task was completed in accordance with the standards you've set up.

	Sun	Mon	Tue	Wed	Thu	Fri	Sat
Make bed							
Brush teeth							
Turn lights off when I leave the room							
Water plants							
Look for scrap paper around house and put in playroom							
Refill bird feeder							
Wash high chair tray							
Shop for an organic fruit to have as snack							
Mail an art project to grandparents							
Wipe down leather couches							

Older children may appreciate a more straightforward "business" approach. Having responsibility makes us feel like a part of the family. It's satisfying to know that we're needed, both in our home and in our community. To the common list of things to do, you may want to add ethical checkpoints. We don't want our children to just rush through chores, seeing them as an obstacle; ideally, we want them to make their beds, fold their clothes, and set the table mindfully. Throwing the comforter up over a "hidden" pile of pillows and pajamas is very different from smoothing down the sheets and making a bed that looks inviting—just as there is a big difference between throwing seeds on the ground and hoping for the best and preparing the soil, properly planting the seeds, and routinely watering the buds. We all deserve a well-made bed, for sleep and for flowers.

Fulfilling our responsibilities with respect for the task at hand has to be taught by example and encouraged through actions. Your child's chore checklist provides a nice opportunity to discuss household and environmental obligations, as well as their ethical implications. Using a wipe board and updating as necessary is an effective practice for household management. Designing a checklist template on your computer and e-mailing that week's goals is an option for tech-savvy families. What should be consistent in either of these approaches is a recurring commitment to performing the responsibilities with integrity. Try adding a code of cleaning conduct to the checklist. A simple statement like, "These chores were completed to the best of my ability. I am proud of the job I did," helps add more meaning to it.

Since taking care of our homes is vital to running a household, I shy away from over-the-top incentives to get kids to do what simply needs to be done. But that doesn't mean that cleaning and taking care of our homes has to be drudgery. Yes, my son loves to squirt his spray bottle, but he doesn't love to pick up his playroom. He would rather keep playing with his toys. For us, the secret is timed transitions and visual aids.

If he's playing and we need to get in the car soon, he gets a five-more-minutes-of-play warning. Then I give him a one-more-minute warning, encouraging him to use his favorite color of Lego or add the last sticker to his art project. When time is up, I bring his shoes into the playroom and tell him, "Mommy is getting ready to go in the car. If you want to come, put your Legos back in the bucket. Bring me your shoes when you're finished and we'll go." The shoes indicate that we're going outside, which he loves to do. I continue getting the baby ready, checking my shopping list, and turning off the lights. If no cleaning up is happening, I walk into the playroom again with my coat on and let him know I'm almost ready; he needs to clean up the Legos. I put one Lego in the bucket, tell him I'm leaving when I get to 10, and start counting. This usually gets things moving. Only once did I have to step outside without him for him to realize I meant business.

If your older children take some poking and prodding to get going, try keeping daily cleaning projects fast and focused. Instead of cleaning the entire house in one day, pick a particular area to focus on. Once there, have your child select his favorite music to play and clean for the duration of the CD. When additional motivation is a must, try setting a timer and beating the clock. Can all the toys be picked up off the floor in under five minutes? Can the laundry be folded and put away before the buzzer sounds? How fast can we unload the dishwasher? Having this age-appropriate aural aid can help keep everyone on track and move chores along with less of an argument. There's a fine line between rushing to get done and doing a job sloppily and focusing on the task at hand for five minutes. In the beginning, model the difference and set up your standards.

Greener Cleaning Products

Right now, when you open up your cleaning cabinet, you're probably greeted by a staggering array of bottles, all claiming to clean, disinfect, sanitize, and leave an area smelling fresh. But what does it really mean to have a clean home?

Isn't it strange that the cleaners we depend on to keep us "healthy" have to be locked away from our children? You would think that *health* was synonymous with *safety*, but when it comes to conventional products, that isn't always the case. On any given day in our country, you'll find parents, employees, and even kids walking around spraying dangerous chemicals on the surfaces we touch, eat off of, and rest on. The same chemicals that help kill germs can hurt humans and pets.

Our obsession with germ-killing formulas has also led to numerous environmental problems. Phosphates used in laundry detergents and dishwasher liquid wreak havoc on rivers and lakes. Almost all cleaners are petroleum based, meaning that this precious nonrenewable resource is literally being flushed down the drain. Chlorine bleach has been linked to cancer in animals and is suspected of contributing to cancer in humans. Bleach is an irritant that can cause breathing difficulty and shouldn't be used by anyone with asthma or respiratory problems. Even worse are the "fresh scent" bleaches that cover up the offensive odor. The odor alerts you that something is wrong; covering it up gives you a false sense of security.

Begin by looking through your own cabinets. You can look for several things to evaluate the safety of the product, and you'll want to dispose of a few things as soon as possible. The most toxic cleaning chemicals are found in drain and oven cleaners and acid-based toilet bowl cleaners. Most of these will be in containers labeled with the words *poison, danger,* or *corrosive*. These words signify a health threat and are far more serious than *caution* or *warning*. Corrosive cleaners can cause burns internally and externally, and are extremely volatile if accidentally mixed with other cleaning agents. If you have these products in your home, it's better to dispose of them than use them. Their ill effects far outweigh any cleaning benefit or financial loss, especially when you consider that there are safe and inexpensive alternatives for all three. These products are considered hazardous materials and must be disposed of properly. Contact your local Department of Public Works to find the nearest safe drop-off center.

Once you rid your cabinets of the dangerous products, you'll also want to find replacements for products that pose potential health and environmental risks. Different cleaning agents, like bleach, ammonia, diethanolamine (DEA), triethanolamine (TEA), ethoxylated alcohols, and other contaminants, have been linked to everything from respiratory problems to cancer. Accidentally mixing bleach and ammonia is a dangerous combination that can result in death. Since manufacturers hold the ingredients of any added fragrances as trade secrets, it's impossible to get a complete picture of what ingredients are mixing together.

As for the environmental implications of commercial cleaners, the damage extends past the container's contents to include the container. Since most detergents are diluted with water before they're packaged in plastic, consumers end up making multiple trips to the store for an environmentally unfriendly product that isn't always recycled. Many households I spoke with admitted that they looked at detergent bottles as garbage, not a recyclable, since the laundry room is farther away from their kitchen's recycling container.

Consumer concern about conventional cleaning products is growing, prompting manufacturers to look for alternative product ingredients that are dependable and effective, and safe for both humans and the environment. Kinder, gentler commercial cleaners are available. Many families are discovering a company that has been in the natural cleaning business for over 50 years: Shaklee. Shaklee products are nontoxic, are formulated without any dangerous chemicals, and come with a 100 percent guarantee, so if you're skeptical that a green cleaner will do the job, you can try these products with no financial risk. Their Get Clean Starter Set includes a variety of products for countertops, windows, and laundry, as well as microfiber cleaning rags. To find a local distributor, visit www.shaklee.net.

If you prefer to pick up your cleaning products at the store, Seventh Generation cleaners are found at most health food stores and select Target retailers. Seventh Generation's products are plant based, not petroleum based, and have no dyes or perfumes. Instead of having a sickly sweet smell or a harsh chemical odor, this line of cleaning products truly smells clean—meaning there's no smell at all!

Do It Yourself

Making your own cleaning products is an easy, inexpensive, and effective way to safely clean your home. No corrosive chemicals, no harsh odors, no dangerous toxins—just all-natural ingredients. A multitude of homemade cleaning combinations are available online, are printed in various books, and, of course, are passed on by word of mouth. Since our goal of going green includes our whole family, I've focused on cleaning ingredients and strategies that are safe for everyone to use. In fact, these cleaners are safe enough to eat!

If you really want to be able to "eat off your floors," it's best to make sure you're cleaning them with edible products. I don't mean to suggest that drinking vinegar and baking soda is a tasty option, but if Junior should knock over the cleaning container, get some solution on his hands, or spray himself in the face, you won't have to call the paramedics. By making your own cleaners, you can reclaim your cabinet space, involve your children in all household cleaning, and breathe easy knowing your house really is clean, not coated with contaminants.

Baking Soda

Everything you need to clean your house can probably be found in your kitchen. The most versatile all-natural cleaning ingredient you need is baking soda. It's a common name for sodium bicarbonate, a natural chemical compound used for maintaining proper pH levels and for baking, as it releases carbon dioxide when heated, causing foods to rise. Since it's a salt, it has a slightly abrasive texture that aids in stain removal and acts as a neutralizer, so odors are eliminated, not just covered up. Many commercial products use baking soda in their formulae, but since they also include chemicals, why not rely solely on the effective cleaning agent and leave the dangerous additives behind? Baking soda can be used on its own or combined with other natural ingredients for tougher jobs.

Five-Minute Makeover

If baking soda needs an extra abrasive boost for tough cleaning jobs, reach for your saltshaker. Salt is an excellent abrasive agent that lends a helpful hand when you risk running out of elbow grease. And since it can easily be diluted with water, it can be used as an effective stain remover when you want a tough job done right but you don't want to scrub. Tea and coffee stains on cups get a lift when you sprinkle salt onto a damp sponge and rub. If you want to clean a tea or coffee pot, fill either pot to capacity, add ¼ cup salt, and boil or percolate as normal. In the warmer months, discard this water outside near your garden to help ward off unwanted pests that dislike salt; in the winter, have your children wash the insides of your windows with the cooled solution to help prevent frost.

If you want to neutralize odors in garbage cans, diaper pails, refrigerators, and carpets, liberally applying baking soda to the offensive area is your best choice. Invite your children to be part of the "Baking Soda Brigade" by trying some of these suggestions. Since kids tend to pour instead of sprinkle, give them the right tools for the job. Fill empty condiment or spice containers with baking soda instead of handing them a box. Mark your new containers and keep one within reach for fast cleanups.

- **Have kids generously sprinkle baking soda on the bottom of the can whenever it's time to take out the trash.** Once a week, add a cup of warm water to baking soda, swish the solution around, empty, and dry.

- **Let it snow in the living room.** First, have the kids broom-sweep the carpeting to loosen dust and dirt from the fibers. Then sprinkle baking soda (snow) all over the rug. Wait 15 minutes and then vacuum for a bright and fresh carpet.

- **Wash the wallpaper.** Dilute ¼ cup of baking soda with a gallon of water in a bucket. Saturate a sponge and wipe down the walls. If the children find a crayon stain or the like, dab baking soda on the area and leave it on for 10 minutes. Then they can wipe away the baking soda and the stain.

- **It's never too early to teach older siblings to help out with a new baby.** Pull a chair up to the sink and have big kids give the baby's bottles and accessories a bath. Add an inch of warm water to the sink and sprinkle in ¼ cup of baking soda. Clean the items inside and out, rinse, and dry. Everything will look and smell like new. Remember, it's a bad idea to put plastics in the dishwasher because high temperatures can cause plastics to leach. Opt for hand washing instead. This system also works for cleaning reusable thermoses.

- **Give stuffed animals a baking soda "spa" treatment.** On a nice day, collect a batch of toys and put them outside on an old sheet. Sprinkle furry friends generously, let them stand for 15 minutes, and then shake the soda off in style. Have family members stand around the perimeter of the sheet and "bounce" the animals around like a game of elementary school parachute. Use your hands to dust off any remaining residue.

- **Send your brigade out to set up baking soda stations throughout your house.** Make soda sachets using mismatched socks, coffee filters tied off with string, or old clothes and sheets cut into fabric squares. Have one child "hide" the sachets behind toilet bowls, in the backs of closets, and near the kitty litter box, keeping track of where the locations are. The following month, have another sibling hunt for the sachets, with you timing her efforts. Note how long the treasure hunt took, and repeat the activity, with the seeker now hiding the sachets for next month's hunt. And don't just throw out the old baking soda. Use it in another way by pouring it into the toilet tank and letting it sit overnight. In the morning, flush and you'll have a clean tank and bowl. If you have a septic tank, this practice will also help you maintain the pH balance and alkalinity, controlling odor.

- **Polish your silverware with a paste made by combining baking soda and water.** Dip a dry rag into the paste and rub it all over the silverware. Rub the "polish" off with a dry rag.

Once you get used to cleaning your home with this fantastic product, you'll want to take it on the road. Teens can care for their cars (or yours) with the help of baking soda. The same silver polish paste can be used to shine hubcaps and chrome bumpers. A sprinkle of baking soda followed by vacuuming can freshen and clean floor mats and interiors. After long road trips, clean bugs and dirt from the windshield by sprinkling baking soda on a damp sponge, rubbing, and rinsing. Keep a box of baking soda in the trunk, with a bag of last season's play sand, to provide traction as necessary on your travels. Stubborn stains on your car, often caused by tree sap or road tar, can be eliminated by applying your baking soda paste to the stain for 10 minutes and then rinsing with a damp sponge. The stain—not the paint—will be gone.

Five-Minute Makeover

After the car is deodorized and cleaned, cut a lemon in half and place each half, flesh side up, in a shallow bowl. Place one lemon bowl on the armrest and one in the trunk overnight to add natural fragrance to your car.

Baking soda is an excellent kitchen and bathroom cleaner. Simply dissolve 2 tablespoons in a quart of water, fill a spray bottle, and clean countertops, toilets, sinks, and showers. If a stain or scratch mark threatens to ruin your counters, try brushing it out with a baking soda paste. Use a tablespoon of your paste and apply to the area with a damp sponge. This paste will also be useful for cleaning in between tile cracks and around faucet handles and sink drains. When trying to remove buildup in these hard-to-reach areas, apply the paste to an old toothbrush and scrub away. (And yes, this same paste can also be used on your own teeth for a natural alternative to commercial brands.) If you need a scouring powder, turn to baking soda again. Sprinkle where needed and clean the area with a damp sponge. Experiment with the amount of baking soda you need to achieve the level of clean you want.

Vinegar

Plain distilled white vinegar is your second must-have household cleaning agent. Its high level of acidity makes it an excellent sanitizing product, effective at killing most germs, bacteria, and mold. Use vinegar to complement other natural products, like baking soda, if you need to disinfect while cleaning. Best of all, vinegar makes chrome, silver, and brass shine. It can safely be used on most surfaces, but you should always spot-test vinegar in an inconspicuous area first to make sure. Never use vinegar on marble; its acidity can ruin it. The best care for marble countertops or floors is preventative. If accidents happen, blot up spills immediately and then wash with clean, soapy water.

One of the banes of my existence is stuck-on price tags. I sometimes think these stickers are affixed with some type of superglue, which is especially problematic if the item is intended as a gift. Saturate the area with vinegar and have your children scrape off tags with a promotional or expired credit card. This is also a great way to remove the last bits of stubborn label paper from glass jars and bottles so you can reuse a more attractive product.

The bathroom and kitchen are two areas where you're probably most concerned about germs. Two parts vinegar and one part water makes for a good all-purpose cleaner. After scouring an area with baking soda on a damp sponge, spray vinegar over it and wipe it down with a dry rag. For cleaning larger areas like floors, fill your kitchen sink halfway using this same formula. Wash the floor and let it air-dry. If you prefer, add the juice of one fresh lemon to the water to leave your floors smelling as good as they look.

Vinegar is great for revitalizing household items you've deemed "goners." The key to salvaging your household items is soaking the stain. Times and techniques may vary, but soaking the stain gives vinegar's acidic properties the chance to go to work loosening the problematic area so you can easily clean it away. Stains, grease build-ups, mineral deposits, and dingy serving platters can all get a much-needed face-lift from vinegar. If the bottoms of your pots and pans tell the story of recipes gone awry, remove the stains by filling them with enough water to entirely cover the stain. Add a cup of vinegar and bring it to a rapid boil for five minutes. Let it cool, and then use a scrubbing sponge to lift the stains. To make the most of your stovetop stain system, put stainless-steel cooking utensils in the pot and clean them at the same time, for a sparkling finish.

Check your recycling container for glass jars whose greasy mayonnaise or jelly remnants discourage you from reusing them. Fill the jars with the vinegar water, adding 2 drops of dishwashing liquid and

1 teaspoon of uncooked rice, to help dislodge remnants, to each. Fit the lids on tightly, shake well, and rinse after 20 minutes for a clean item ready to be reused. Before you give up on your things, give them a vinegar treatment. Save the product and take a step toward saving Earth.

Showerheads can also benefit from a vinegar treatment. Fill your kitchen sink halfway with one part vinegar to two parts warm water. Unscrew all your showerheads at once and soak them for 20 minutes. Have your children use an old toothbrush to brush away loosened mineral deposits. Next, clean hard-to-reach places like between Venetian blind slats by having them slip on a pair of cotton gloves and dip their fingers in the water. And they can saturate those gloved hands in water, and shake off the excess. Take an extra-healthy step by wiping down the bottoms of all the family's shoes to remove winter rock salt, summer pesticides, dirt, and grime. Gloved hands help you get in between a shoe's treads. When you're done, remove the gloves and wash your hands with soap and water, and dry thoroughly to remove the vinegar smell.

Five-Minute Makeover

If your children reach for their paintbrushes only to find the bristles stuck together because they forgot to rinse them, tell them to get the vinegar. Pour a little into a cup and let the brushes sit in the liquid for five minutes. Then massage the bristles and rinse the brushes in a cup of warm water. Repeat the process until the bristles are free and clean.

Lemons

If you love the smell of a lemon-fresh house, add a fresh lemon to your natural cleaners. Roll a lemon under your palm to loosen the fruit from the skin, cut it in half, and squeeze the juice into your spray bottle of vinegar or baking soda. Lemon is a disinfectant that helps kill germs while it freshens the air. It can also be used alone or combined with olive oil. Keep in mind, though, that young children tend to be covered with scratches and cuts that lemon juice would irritate. If your children are prone to nicks and scrapes, dilute lemon juice into a solution first, or make sure your kids wear dishwashing gloves.

Your kitchen cutting boards are a haven for smelly bacteria. Help sanitize them and rid them of unwanted odors by cutting a lemon in half and placing it cut side down on the board. Rub the lemon over the board, squeezing as you go. Then rinse with cool water. When finished, squeeze any remaining juice onto a clean, damp sponge and leave it in the refrigerator for several hours to absorb odors while freshening. If you have one, put lemon peels in your garbage disposal to clean and freshen, or toss them into your fireplace at the beginning of the season to help rid the hearth of damp and musty smells.

If you find yourself throwing out reusable plastic containers because they just don't look clean, look to a lemon for help. You can remove food stains on plastic by squeezing a fresh lemon into the stained container and adding a tablespoon of baking soda and enough water to cover the stain. Let soak overnight and rinse in the morning.

Looking for a good polish for your wood furniture? Mix two parts olive oil with one part lemon juice in a spray bottle. This solution can also help restore luster to leather furniture; just be sure to spot test an inconspicuous area first. This cleaner works wonders on car interiors, helping "kid-friendly" cars clean up nicely.

Five-Minute Makeover

As you learn more about do-it-yourself home-cleaning products, you're likely to come upon recipes that include Borax. Borax is a good alternative for people who are used to using bleach. It can be mixed with vinegar to disinfect and clean the stubborn stains that form in toilet bowl rings or grout. Although it's a natural mineral and environmentally friendly, it can be toxic if ingested, so I haven't chosen to recommend it in this chapter. If you'd like to have Borax on hand for problem areas, keep it in a safe spot if you have children. A quick all-purpose cleaner using Borax is one part Borax to three parts vinegar. Borax is also commonly used to give soap a boost in cleaning power.

You'll find that these everyday kitchen products can work wonders throughout your home. Since your whole family can now contribute to cleaning, you can feel good knowing your revamped cleaning practices are part of your overall eco-friendly goals, gentler on your wallet and the environment.

Cleansing Your Home

Cleaning is about more than ridding a home of germs. It's also about making an environment warm and inviting. Many eco-friendly families also appreciate the mind, body, spirit connection. While cleaning traditionally focuses on keeping our bodies germ-free, our discussion has touched upon purposeful cleaning and ways to help children (and ourselves) see the connection between a clean home and a clean planet. To do this effectively, we can look at some simple ways to cleanse our homes.

Walk into each room of your house and ask yourself these questions:

- When I enter this room, what's my first reaction? (Relief? Despair? Frustration? Calm?)
- After being in this room for a period of time, how do I feel? (Relief? Despair? Frustration? Calm?)
- Is this room doing what it is intended to?
- Am I productive in the laundry room?
- Are we rested in the bedrooms?
- Are we creative in the playroom?
- Am I satisfied in the kitchen?

Cleansing our home means rebalancing the energy so it feels like it's working with us, not against us. How many times have I yelled at the jammed kitchen drawer because it wouldn't open, only to find it filled with personal items that I've hidden in there? Becoming angry and frustrated in the very same room where I make the food that's supposed to nurture my family is a contradiction.

Decluttering work spaces makes us more productive. You'll find that when you're focused, you lose track of time. You become so engaged with the task at hand that you stop checking the clock and lose yourself in the project, emerging energized and rested. I find that true when I'm scrapbooking or writing. When I'm not distracted by empty drinking glasses, unopened mail, and puzzle pieces on my desk, I work much more efficiently. When my bedroom is tidy, I have an easier time falling asleep. Decluttering helps make each room more purposeful.

Young children may not be able to answer those questions, but their behavior is indicative of their experience. When our playroom is cluttered and neglected, the boys are unfocused; they run about and are argumentative. When the bedrooms are strewn with laundry that hasn't been put away and toys that have been left out, and beds have been unmade, it takes much longer to settle down. Tweens and teens, however, can be walked through the list and share their answers. When it's taking especially long to put laundry away, finish homework, or get the dinner table set, it could be because clothes are piling up, desks are being used as a dumping ground, and the kitchen space is overwhelmed with projects and paperwork.

Everyone can benefit from decluttering. Take a moment to move things into their rightful places. Play "hunter and gatherer" with younger children by setting a timer for five minutes. Give each child an empty laundry basket to fill with all the miscellaneous things that are cluttering the room. In the playroom, random game pieces, stuffed animals, and snack dishes can be piled into the basket. Once everything is hunted and gathered and the buzzer has sounded, reset the timer for 15 minutes, instructing kids to return the items to their proper places.

For your older children, decluttering usually means taking inventory, assessing the things that surround them, and streamlining. Using three laundry baskets marked "Yes," "No," and "Maybe," teens can go through their rooms and sort through all the things they've accumulated. Once the baskets are filled, "Yes" items are put away properly, "No" items are taken into a common area to be reused and recycled, and "Maybe" items are left in the basket for 48 hours. If nothing from the basket is retrieved, the contents are reused by other family members or are recycled.

Five-Minute Makeover

To cut down on stair time, we keep a bedtime basket on the steps. If a bedroom stuffed animal or toy has made its way downstairs to the playroom, my son can take it to the stairs when we're cleaning up. The next time we head upstairs, we grab the basket and make better use of our time.

After decluttering, you can address any lingering negative energy. Children will especially enjoy making their personal spaces more friendly. Negative energy can be lingering in a room that was decluttered but hasn't been enjoyed in quite some time. It can result from too many days spent housebound in cold winter months, when everyone finds themselves short on patience. It can accumulate after a particularly stressful time at work or school, when too many hours are spent getting professional projects completed or studying for midterms, and things feel out of balance. Or it can be a lasting feeling of lethargy after family members have been ill. Getting the house's spirit back in balance helps everyone feel more centered.

The activities used to balance a home are also beneficial for our environment. All too often we use "retail therapy" to cure our blues. While a new toy or new purse may temporarily lift our spirits, that's really a Band-Aid on the symptom instead of a cure for the problem: burnout. The more we buy, the more resources we use. It may be a new concept to think of less as more, but taking simple steps to make a home more streamlined can boost everyone's spirits without straining any eco-resources.

If you want to shake the uncomfortable feeling in your home and get everyone on track, you can do some simple things. These ideas can be used as an on-the-spot treatment when it seems the home is under a "black cloud" or as a seasonal project to clear your house of stale energy and welcome in a new year—maybe September's school year or January's calendar year—or a new season. After a good housecleaning and houseclearing, enjoy a house cleansing with these family-friendly activities:

- **Weather permitting, open all the windows and doors.**
  Nothing helps clear the air in your home like actual fresh air.
  Throw open all the windows and doors, and let the sun shine
  in as the wind whips about. Walk with your young children and
  plant your feet in the center of each room, raising your arms
  above your heads. Take deep breaths in and out while your
  arms wave in the breeze like tree branches. This activity always
  ends up with my older son spinning around in a fit of giggles.
  There isn't a product on the market that can bottle that kind of
  positive energy. When your fresh-air walk is finished, close the
  doors and the majority of windows, leaving one or two open as
  a reminder of your activity.

- **Salt, an excellent cleaning agent, is also a beneficial cleansing tool, used in many detoxifying scrubs.** "Scrub" your
  problem area by making a salt sachet. Fill a mismatched sock
  with a tablespoon of salt and wipe down furniture and walls,
  then place it in the corner of a room that's been particularly
  troublesome. For us, that means scrubbing the playroom, which
  can easily become overly chaotic. Leave the sachet in the corner
  overnight and discard it in the morning. If family members are
  personally struggling with a streak of bad luck, a salt shower
  can be a symbolic way to wash away negative energy.

- **Create music.** If it seems that your home is too noisy (with
  yelling, punishments, and whining or crying being the order of
  the day), change the atmosphere by creating music for your ears.
  Wind chimes are melodic, giving everyone the opportunity to
  hear something soothing. This easy-to-make wind chime uses
  materials you probably have on hand.

4 clean aluminum cans
1 spoon
Empty oatmeal container
String, yarn, or ribbon
Rubber bands
Hole punch
Construction paper
Crayons, markers, glitter, glue
Scissors

1. Remove the lid from an oatmeal box and punch four holes around the circumference of the container, spacing the holes evenly.

2. Lace a piece of string through each hole so two ends hang down from each opening.

3. Flip over the container and score two parallel holes in the bottom of the corner, about 1 inch apart. Coming up through the inside of the container, lace a piece of string through the hole, making sure the two ends are long enough to hang out of the bottom. Tie the handle of the spoon to the string so it hangs.

4. Score two more holes on the bottom of the container, this time at the outer edges. Lace a string through the holes and tie off. This loop will be used to hang your finished wind chime.

5. Turn four clean cans upside down and secure a rubber band around the can, a quarter of the way from the top. Using the string from one hole, slip an end under the band on one side of the can, and an end under the band on the other side, leaving enough room to tie off. This will secure the can to the oatmeal container. Repeat this three more times, securing all cans.

6. Use construction paper to decorate the container, by either coloring or cutting out shapes. Glue to oatmeal box.

7. Hang near an open window and enjoy your musical creation.

If your teen is going through a tough time, but a homemade craft seems too childish, use ingredients from your kitchen to cleanse and reenergize an area. If procrastination is preventing her from getting that project completed, turn to sage, which is said to clear away stale energy. Sprinkle dry leaves in a shallow dish and set it on the corner of her desk. If an audition, public speaking event, or interview is on the horizon, trust thyme to inspire courage. The night before the event, pour boiling water into a mug filled with ¼ teaspoon dried thyme leaves. Place the steeping mug on the nightstand and inhale fragrant tea while sleeping. Should a broken heart or bad argument with a close friend weigh down your child, help her heal with a fresh lemon and salt bath. Fill a tub with warm water and add 2 tablespoons of salt, a detoxifier, and the juice of one fresh squeezed lemon, a cleansing agent. Soaking in this solution can help teens emerge feeling relaxed and relieved.

In addition, if teens are distracted and have a project that must be completed, suggest they place garden stones in their pockets to help ground them. Make sure a healthy potted plant like English ivy, as mentioned in Chapter 3, is placed in the corner of a room to help remove lingering toxins from the air. Try rearranging bedroom furniture to shake things up and give a personal space a fresh perspective.

Cleansing our personal spaces of negative energy is just as important to our health as cleaning our homes of germs. Just as germs can make us feel sick, bad energy can weigh us down. Taking steps to promote our physical and emotional health helps to ensure that we'll be able to stick with our eco-friendly plans. The healthier we feel physically and the more clearheaded we are mentally, the more likely we are to appreciate the gifts of our environment and make every effort to preserve these resources.

Chapter Checklist

☐ We will personalize individual cleaning buckets and all have an active role in household maintenance.

☐ We will design and abide by a cleaning code of conduct.

☐ We will make a natural all-purpose cleaner using baking soda and vinegar.

☐ We will have fun cleaning, knowing that taking care of our personal environment is a way of taking care of our global environment.

☐ We will cleanse our home, not just clean it.

Marking Milestones: Birthdays and Beyond

Despite my best green intentions, it's hard not to get caught up in the commercialism of special occasions like holidays and birthdays. I grew up in a family that placed an important emphasis on gift giving. Unfortunately, there was an unspoken understanding that the bigger and better the gift, the more valued you were. Homemade gifts were unheard of; we drove to megamalls and superstores, and paid top dollar for that season's must-have item.

This skewed approach to gift giving extended to baby showers, graduations, and housewarmings. Instead of celebrating the person or his achievements, the focus was on the gift giver. The emphasis wasn't on time spent with friends and family; it was a gift-wrapped competition.

When I had my own children, I wanted to change this pattern. I had to rethink what I wanted celebrating and commemorating to mean to my own family. Just as I learned that there were alternatives to conventional medicines, foods, and cleaning products, I learned there were greener gift-giving ideas available. Yes, we still purchase gifts from stores, but those gifts round out our holidays and celebrations; they aren't the main focus. We've expanded our idea of what commemorating special occasions means, whether planning for the holiday season or planning a family vacation. Our emphasis is on time and energy spent on each other, with special efforts being made to honor and appreciate the people we care about.

Guests of Honor

We have numerous opportunities to celebrate those we hold near and dear to our hearts. Traditional calendars are dotted with predetermined times to see friends and family. Add to this our own personal timeline of events, and it's likely that you could easily become overwhelmed by your obligations. For so many, holidays and birthdays have become a source of stress instead of celebration, with too much time being spent on shopping and event planning. But it doesn't have to be that way.

When we keep the focus on the guest of honor instead of becoming sidetracked by expensive presents, we not only increase the likelihood of keeping a level head and enjoying special occasions, but we also keep our eco-friendly efforts on track. The most meaningful gift we could give any friend or relative is the gift of our time. With so many families adhering to such busy schedules, carving out uninterrupted time with someone special is among the best ways to honor that person.

One of the easiest ways to present someone with an invitation to spend time together is to customize a gift certificate. Children of all ages can construct this present, with abilities dictating how elaborate the project can get. Young children can fasten together strips of construction paper to create a "coupon book" of activities to enjoy with their gift recipient. Ideas could include anything from a game of checkers to raking leaves together. Wrapping and presenting this gift to a family member, especially grandparents, is a wonderful way to create memories, the best gift of all.

Tweens and teens could elaborate on this gift idea and make coupon books or specialized gift certificates for teachers and neighbors. Volunteering to help a teacher create a bulletin board or organize bookshelves after school would be greatly appreciated. Helping an elderly neighbor save money and energy by "greening" her home through cleaning refrigerator coils, making door socks, or checking the car's tire pressure takes eco-friendly gift giving to the next level. Not only are children avoiding resource-depleting commercial products, but they're further implementing the important eco-friendly lifestyle you're all committed to at home.

Taking an active interest in the causes that are important to the person you are celebrating is another wonderful way to honor someone. A beloved aunt who is an active member of the Rotary Club would greatly appreciate having your family volunteer at the next event. A cousin who is dedicated to animal welfare would be honored if you dropped off blankets to the shelter where she works on the weekend. More than just a donation of money, these gifts take energy and enthusiasm to implement. Doing so is another way to celebrate someone while helping to make your local community—and, by extension, the global community—a better place to live.

Thinking Outside the Gift Box

If distance or conflicting schedules make it too difficult to plan a one-on-one visit, some presents can be personalized across the miles. Reading aloud can work for the youngest and oldest of gift recipients. Although children's picture books are available on tape, hearing an older cousin's voice read a favorite story would be a much more pleasant surprise. If your tween has outgrown a tape player or no longer uses a headset, this is a great opportunity to breathe new life into a handed-down gift. Older relatives who can no longer enjoy reading because of poor eyesight would love the company of a book and a familiar voice on tape, too.

Plan accordingly for these long-distance gifts, giving yourself ample time to mail presents. It's better to send a gift early with a message on the box that reads "Do not open until the morning of your birthday" than to have to pay overnight delivery and unintentionally sabotage your good green efforts by using the additional precious natural resources needed to rush your delivery.

If these options don't seem feasible, donating to an organization like Heifer International is a powerful eco-friendly gift. Its slogan, "Ending Hunger, Caring for the Earth," is put into practice by helping families around the world learn how to become self-sustaining. Its one-of-a-kind online catalog allows you to choose to fund sheep, water buffalo, ducks, and other life-sustaining livestock for poor villages throughout the world. Your donation helps Heifer International teach villagers how to raise livestock, making it possible to end poverty, not just temporarily treat it. A downloadable gift card lets you personalize a message to the friend or family member you are honoring with this contribution. For more information, visit www.heifer. org.

While we tend to think of gift giving as a joyous occasion, commemorating someone's life after they've died is another admirable way to celebrate a loved one. At our area's Community Supported Garden, donations can be made to the Memorial Garden, a beautiful field of wildflowers. What better way is there to celebrate someone's life than by honoring them in a blooming garden? Planting flowers or trees in someone's name can be a comfort to those family members who are left behind and can serve as a beautiful reminder that those who are gone are not forgotten.

Hassle-Free Homemade Gifts

Setting ourselves up for a successful year of holidays and special occasions takes some preplanning, but the payoff is financially, emotionally, and environmentally beneficial.

Using a daily planner or your home computer, look at a blank calendar copy of the upcoming year. Mark every gift-giving occasion you can think of, from holidays to anniversaries, birthdays, and graduations, and you'll quickly find that your calendar is filled with important dates. Chances are, however, this honest effort is incomplete, since it will be impossible to guesstimate your children's friends' birthday parties or various other occasions you'll be invited to celebrate (and feel obligated to bring a gift to). Planning now for upcoming celebrations, both planned and spontaneous, can help you and your families become greener gift givers.

Homemade gifts are at the top of my green present list, but many families are reluctant to go this route, concerned that the gifts will take too long, fall short of the mark, or not measure up to store-bought items. Luckily, several everyday ideas can be put together with minimum time and energy, and would be a welcome addition to any celebration. Most important, all of these ideas have the environment in mind, meaning that you can make your guests of honor feel good about their special day while you feel good about your eco-friendly choices.

Keeping gifts on hand offers several green benefits. Nurturing mini herb gardens in the fall in anticipation of holiday hostess gifts is very different from racing around on Christmas Eve, hoping a personalized gift can be ready by daybreak. Families who enjoy making things together will appreciate accomplishing two tasks, a hands-on activity and a personalized gift, at once. Since these projects can be made before they're actually needed, you end up building time into your schedule, making it less likely that you'll have to depend on environmentally depleting methods like overnight shipping from a catalog or isolated car trips in search of one present. And, of course, these ideas promote greener living for both the giver and the receiver, making them projects that naturally fit into your eco-friendly lifestyle.

Of course, the holiday season is usually the busiest time for gift giving. In addition to the other crafts and gift-giving ideas throughout this book, here are ideas for homemade holidays. You can do all of these things well in advance of the winter, making them great rainy-day activity ideas to capture your children's imagination. Even kids who would usually prefer electronics over these energy-saving projects are more likely to participate, knowing they're making a gift.

Five-Minute Makeover

Give the gift of reusable bags. As discussed in Chapter 4, many supermarkets have begun selling their own brand of reusable bags. Help spread your eco-efforts by purchasing several bags to keep on hand to give as a housewarming present or hostess gift. Fold up the bags and place them inside one opened bag, recycle a colorful ribbon from home, and give a gift that makes errands easier and helps the environment.

Festive Placemats

Recyclable computer paper with one side used
Construction paper with artwork on one side
Various fruits and vegetables
Paint
Glue
Raffia (optional)

Glue computer paper, used side facedown, to the back of construction paper and let dry. Cut fruits and vegetables to expose insides and paint various colors. If you cut an apple in half, you'll find a star shape. Carrots make great dots and are easy for little hands to manage. For added decoration, punch a hole on each end and tie raffia bows at the ends. Give a collection of place mats as a hostess gift.

Rock Place Settings

Different sizes of rocks
Various decoration scraps: ribbon, fabric scraps, googly eyes, and more

This gift can be hilarious for older kids to make. First, pick out a rock to represent a family member; then decorate it to resemble that person. Long hair? Glasses? Tie? Set the table with these personalities and enjoy a good laugh. These are a fun party favor to make if you're hosting a holiday meal.

Detergent Snowman

Detergent flakes
Water
Various craft materials: foam, ribbon, beans, and more
Glue
Craft/popsicle sticks
Plastic gloves (for those with sensitive skin)

This is an eco-friendly way to use up your phosphate detergent flakes. Mix flakes and water until a puddinglike consistency forms. You'll have to play around with this until you get the consistency you want; different brands yield different results.

Form three "snowballs" and stack them. Insert a stick from top to bottom through the middle to help it stand. While it's drying, decorate it with bean eyes, a foam nose, craft stick arms, a ribbon scarf, or other materials, using glue, if necessary, to keep items in place. Let dry overnight.

Recycled Holiday Village

Empty boxes of various sizes
Construction paper
Glue
Miscellaneous decorative pieces
Cotton balls

Gather empty boxes—assorted pasta boxes work great—and completely cover them with construction paper. Add windows, doors, and other features. Stretch out the cotton balls and glue the "snow" on roofs, sidewalks, and other areas. A great gift idea is to "design" your own house (or Grandma's) and decorate it accordingly—a personalized snow village house.

Oatmeal Cookie Container

Empty oatmeal cookie container
Construction paper
Batch of cookies
Miscellaneous decorative pieces

Cover the container with white construction paper and decorate a snowman face. Bake a batch of oatmeal raisin cookies and place them inside the waxed paper-lined container.

Winter Mosaic

Styrofoam pieces
Beans
Glue
Paintbrush

This is a great project to work on after the holidays, as you are likely to have shipping Styrofoam on hand that you'll want to reuse. Cut the pieces to a desired size and cover them with a thin layer of glue. Use multicolored beans to create a snow scene, a flower design, or the recipient's initials. Let dry completely, then brush a thin layer of glue over the whole project to secure. Let dry completely.

Snowman Kit

Unmatched and/or outgrown hats, gloves, and scarves
Sticks from the yard
Coal or garden rocks

Gather all the makings of a snowman (or snow family, if you're feeling really ambitious) and wrap them up in a box. Write out the steps for a snowman-making fun day. For example:

1. Daddy makes his world-famous pancakes for breakfast.
2. We all put on our winter coats and head outside.
3. Roll three huge snowballs ....
4. Decorate ....
5. Celebrate with Mommy's first-class hot chocolate.

You can make this as simple or as involved as you want.

Little Hands Bookmarks

Construction paper creations
Crayons/markers
Clear packing tape
Hole punch, ribbon

Use your toddler's artwork to create one-of-a-kind bookmarks. Cut the art into thick strips of paper. "Laminate" with packing tape. Use a hole punch at the top of each strip and tie off with ribbon.

You may be surprised by how much everyone in your family will enjoy making these gifts. When we embrace the holidays as a season for celebrating family instead of just a time for getting presents, we're more likely to come away with memories, not migraines.

Celebrating Eco-Babies

Some of my favorite people in the world to honor are new parents. The anticipation and arrival of a new baby is such an exciting time for everyone. Many of us, myself included, trust baby superstores to furnish us with all the essentials, only to find that what we think we need and what we actually end up using are two different things entirely. Knowing the difference can help new parents be better prepared for their bundle of joy and help your family share their joy of greener living. Consider giving new families the gift of T.I.M.E., with handmade thank-you cards, information about local resources, meals that are nutritious and tasty, and encouragement during an uncertain time.

Thank-You Cards

When a new bundle of joy arrives, so do the well-wishers. Help a new mom show her appreciation by designing a ready-made basket of gratitude. Have your children decorate plain cardstock paper, available at craft stores, to use as one-of-a-kind thank-you cards. Provide matching envelopes and stamps, and present them in a reusable basket with pens. You'll give your friend a convenient way to express her thanks, leaving her more time to enjoy her gifts with her new baby.

Information

There are dozens of things to learn about raising an eco-baby, but with midnight feedings and loads of laundry taking precedence over green research, new parents can struggle over sorting through the information. Help spread the word about eco-friendly living by creating a green notebook. Reusing an old school notebook, fill in the remaining pages with green tips and suggestions your family has incorporated into daily life. From turning out the lights when you leave a room to washing baby's clothes in baking soda, this personalized notebook can be decorated and designed with a new baby's needs in mind.

Meals

Good nutrition, which should be a top priority for growing families, tends to take a backseat to convenience foods when sleep-deprived parents are trying to get dinner on the table. Delivering premade meals like casseroles prepared with organic vegetables can provide a generous and healthy dinner the first night, with leftovers covering lunch the next day. Cooking with kids and sharing your creations with friends and family is a gift that everyone can enjoy.

Encouragement

The arrival of a new baby brings an onslaught of instant relatives, but visits tend to thin out a few weeks after the big day. Let new parents know you're thinking about them by mailing thoughtful cards and creations. If the budding artist in your home has painted several self-portraits, mail the masterpiece with a note. Older children can send jokes, poems, or new recipes in the mail as a way of staying connected to busy families without being a burden.

Five-Minute Makeover

Before hitting the stores, ask yourself if there's an antique or collectible you can pass along to an expanding family. When my grandmother died, she left me several of her embroidered hankies. I made sure to pack one in my hospital bag and tuck it into my newborn son's bassinet as a reminder of her. When my best friend became pregnant, I sent her a treasured handkerchief as a reminder of all the mothers we have watching over us. She was so moved by this unexpected, heartfelt gift that she added the memento to her daughter's keepsake box.

If you'd prefer to give a more traditional gift instead of, or in addition to, the gift of T.I.M.E., the store-bought gifts you choose don't have to compromise your green ideals. I was fortunate to meet several small business owners at our Holistic Moms National Conference this year and talked with them about the products they carry. Babies, and the gifts we give them, have become a billion-dollar business. Baby supplies have gone beyond the basics, to include professionally designed nurseries with color-coordinated accessories and furniture, all bestowed upon an expectant mother at her elaborate baby shower. While no one would argue with honoring a new mother, making a big fuss over a baby's arrival, or getting something special for a first birthday present, the small business owners I spoke with have opted to honor mother, baby, and the planet by providing products that are eco-friendly. Seeking out companies like these makes eco-conscious consumerism possible and helps pass along your good eco-intentions to a whole new generation.

Amy Biasucci owns and operates Acorn, a storefront and website business. All of Amy's products are made by ecologically and socially responsible companies that use natural fibers and organic materials that are never tested on animals. Her adorable apparel line includes green items like her own "Contains No Artificial Sweeteners" toddler T-shirt design, printed on 100 percent organic cotton. This mom-owned business can be found at www.acornplace.com.

Heather Anderson, president and founder of Blessed Nest, Inc., has found a way to make a nursery staple more functional and environmentally responsible. Her all-organic Nesting Pillows help pregnant women find a comfortable, supported resting position; provide flexible assistance when breastfeeding; and can later be used by babies for tummy time or enjoyed by toddlers when relaxing with books or watching a movie. The options are endless. I love this product because it grows with your family, making it a handmade gift that will be appreciated for years to come. Giving sustainable and practical presents that are handmade in the United States under fair and favorable working conditions using beautiful organic materials represents the best green consumerism has to offer. Visit the company at www.blessednest.com.

If you're looking for a really great green alternative to traditional wishing wells, you might appreciate Kristin Rainey's idea. As the owner of Little Willow, Kristin sells cloth diapers and also helps baby shower hostesses coordinate with guests, who are encouraged to each buy one diaper for the new parents. Since partygoers may not know how or where to find these products, Little Willow makes it easy to give a great green gift. For a wide selection of cloth diaper options and other simple, natural products, visit www.littlewillowbaby.com.

In addition to the companies profiled here, you can find more environmentally friendly businesses and sustainable goods in the eco-marketplace appendix at the end of this book.

Greener Party Planning

Special occasions have become an additional source of strain on natural resources. For starters, many celebratory parties depend on disposable cutlery, plates, and serving platters. Not having enough dishware on hand to host a large gathering, wanting to keep cleanup simple, or opting for a character-inspired children's theme party, we buy one-time-use products that end up in the garbage after a few short hours. We offer guests bottles of water and send them home with a plastic goody bag filled with plastic trinkets. But there's a better way to balance festive decorations and easy entertaining with environmental savvy. Regardless of the occasion, everyone in the family can help plan, decorate, and host a special event in your home. The keys to green hosting are using what you have on hand, choosing eclectic over monochromatic, and asking for help so you can enjoy a special occasion without breaking the bank or breaking your commitment to eco-friendly living.

If you're hosting your child's birthday party, for example, and he wants everything to be SpongeBob, use the toys you already have as decorations. The birthday boy can round up every SpongeBob stuffed toy, T-shirt, and pillowcase he has and bring them into the area where you will be hosting. Once there, use the T-shirts to cover the chairs, tie stuffed toys together with a big ribbon to use as a centerpiece, and set up pillowcases for a potato sack race. Cut your yellow kitchen sponges into different sea shapes and lay out brown grocery bags for decorating. During the party, guests can create sponge-painted sea scene crafts that can also double as party favors.

Continue to plan activities and snacks using what you already have on hand, and you'll find that you don't need a lot of expensive, disposable plastic items to create the theme you want. Any cartoon character or beloved stuffed animal can become the focus of your theme party. For added fun, you can invite children to bring their own stuffed guest of honor to the party, and play games like Hide-and-Go-Seek with the toys.

For larger gatherings, invite guests to be a part of the party planning. For our Holistic Moms chapter children's holiday party, each family signed up to bring a healthy dish to share; came with their own plates, cups, and cutlery; and brought markers, crayons, and miscellaneous craft materials for an activity. The emphasis was on celebrating with friends in a relaxed atmosphere, not staging an elaborate and stuffy event that would have exhausted the hostess and gone unappreciated by the toddlers. The eclectic collection of tableware and foods made a festive and funky table that was functional for our energetic crowd.

Five-Minute Makeover

Private parties aren't the only get-togethers going green. More major corporations are taking steps to host more environmentally sustainable events. Wells Fargo, the country's leading diversified financial company, has committed to going green by hosting more environmentally responsible business meetings. Pitchers of water have replaced plastic bottles; agendas are posted in central locations, eliminating multiple paper copies of the same information; and signs are designed to be used again and again. Wells Fargo was the only financial institution to receive a 2007 Green Power Partner of the Year award from the U.S. Environmental Protection Agency (EPA) for its leadership in the green power market, having purchased billions of kilowatt-hours of green power. If you want to green your green, visit www.wellsfargo.com.

The same mismatched settings could work perfectly for a more formal tea, where individual tea cups and china would provide a lovely conversation piece. As guests arrive, you could ask each one to place her cup, saucer, and plate at a table decorated with flowers from your garden and books from your shelves. Before sitting down, have guests draw numbers out of a teapot, with #1 being the first person to choose where to sit. The only rule? You can't choose your own dishes! This icebreaker is a great way for acquaintances to get to know each other and a terrific way for the hostess to avoid problematic plastic dishes.

Finally, ask for help. If you hate the idea of your party being mismatched, or if asking guests to supply their own dishes isn't possible, consider contacting a caterer who's likely to have a large number of matching serving dishes and linens. For our chapter's "Moms Only" party, we opted to use a caterer who supplied china, glasses, and linens at no additional cost so we could all enjoy a night off while not sacrificing our eco-mindedness. The caterer, an equally environmentally minded individual, was happy to hear that we were a "green group." Likewise, I was thrilled to find someone so accommodating and am happy to refer On Call Caterers in Flanders, New Jersey, to my area friends and family. This is a win/win/win situation, with guests, purveyor, and environment benefiting.

When it's time for your guests to leave, think about offering them a party favor that does Earth a favor, too. You can pass along several inexpensive, eco-friendly things to express your gratitude and your greenness. When an event is on the horizon, begin looking around your home for items you have in excess or things you simply aren't using. For us right now, it's baby food jars. For your family, it could be cardboard toilet paper holders, old plastic water bottles (on hand before you switched to a reusable thermos), tea bags you bought on sale but still haven't used, or a hand-me-down collection of antique teaspoons that are just sitting in a drawer. Look for creative, simple ways to make the most of what you already have.

- **Here's another idea for your SpongeBob Party.** Consider filling empty water bottles with 1 to 2 cups sand, summer sea-shells, gummy fish, and water mixed with blue food coloring for a personalized "aquarium."

- **Baby food jars make excellent votive candle holders.** Fill jars a quarter of the way with salt, add a pinch of glitter, and then shake to mix. Place a votive candle in the middle of the salt to secure it, close the cap, and cover the top with a decorative fabric square kept in place with a rubber band. Cover the rubber band with a piece of ribbon and give these favors out at a holiday gathering.

- **Make special tea party favors.** Guests will enjoy taking home an antique spoon, a tea bag, and a honey stick, tied together with a ribbon. Instead of sitting in a drawer, your collection will receive the attention it deserves and become a lovely keepsake from an enjoyable afternoon.

- **Find a new use for toilet tissue rolls.** Fill them with candy, stickers, seed packets, or small crayons, and wrap them in anything from bandanas to the Sunday comics. These treasures can be tied to any party theme.

Once you open yourself up to the possibility of greener hosting options, your whole family will enjoy coming up with clever themes, games, and keepsakes to celebrate special events.

Five-Minute Makeover

I'm a huge fan of regifting and see it as another opportunity to reuse items I have on hand instead of tapping into new resources. When friends, family, and clients give me gifts I can't use, like perfumed candles that aggravate our family's allergies, I can graciously accept the gift and pass it on to someone who will actually enjoy it. Regifting isn't bad manners. In my green opinion, throwing out perfectly useful items or stashing them in the back of the closet and buying new things is much more socially inappropriate.

Vacation Destination

Taking a break from the hustle and bustle of your family's busy routine doesn't have to mean breaking away from your eco-friendly lifestyle. Since going green is a family affair, it makes sense to take your eco-friendly habits on the road with you. Whether you're planning an afternoon excursion or packing luggage to last you for a week, traveling down greener roads is fun and easy.

You can have an ideal eco-trip right in your own backyard. Becoming a temporary tourist in your own town is an inexpensive way to take advantage of local points of interest, uses considerably less gas than a long-distance trip, and offers the opportunity to connect with community members. When we live close to museums, monuments, or mountain ranges, we tend to take those things for granted, assuming that we can always see them, while arranging for a trip elsewhere. Unfortunately, we often end up putting off local visits indefinitely. I grew up in New York but regret to say I've never visited the Statue of Liberty. While it's a trip I plan to take with my own children, I'm disappointed I haven't been there yet. Even if such tourist spots aren't in your neck of the woods, there are still dozens of things to do in your neighborhood. If you need help getting started, check out *The Complete Idiot's Guide to Backyard Adventures* by Nancy Worrell for great ideas.

Five-Minute Makeover

Day trips are a great way to have fun as a family. Before you head out on a road trip, be sure to revisit the suggestions on getting your car tuned-up for your trip in Chapter 4. Check the air pressure, oil, and fluids, and address any maintenance issues before you leave home, to help ensure a safer and greener trip.

As you prepare to play tourist, look for ways to make the occasion even more eco-friendly. Pack your own lunch, bring along reusable bags to collect treasures, and take public transportation or ride your bikes. Resist the urge to get other errands done along the way, and instead enjoy your vacation day. Turn off your cell phone, skip e-mail, and turn off the TV. Try any one of these fun and easy "vacation" ideas and take in the sights:

1. Visit the library for a book on trees, and take a walk through your neighborhood to identify leaves.

2. Contact your area's historical society or chamber of commerce, and inquire about local history. Many towns have homes that have been registered as historical landmarks and are available for viewing with advance notice.

3. Order the lunch special from a local eatery and eat in the park.

4. Take a walk in the rain and see how different your town looks in this weather.

5. Arrange for a family field trip through the post office, supermarket, or bank, and learn how things work "behind the scenes."

6. Fill a knapsack with scrap paper, crayons, and markers, and find a quiet corner to sketch a lovely local scene, like an old bridge, a calm pond, or an interesting tree.

7. Call local college theaters or town playhouses, and reserve seats at an upcoming performance.

Deciding where to go on your trip can be almost as fun as the trip itself. Since you don't have to make a deposit on a room, make reservations, or stick to an itinerary, you can let the kids take a more active role in planning your trip. They can brainstorm a list of local places they want to know more about and the family can choose from it, or you can pick an idea out of a hat for even more spontaneity. Siblings may enjoy taking turns planning these day trips, deciding when and wear to have lunch or how long to spend at the museum. Following our children's lead and respecting how they want to spend their time is a great way to honor their opinion while learning more about their interests.

The Beauty of Bartering

Family-focused volunteer tourism is growing in popularity, with organizations like Earthwatch and the Sierra Club inviting enthusiastic environmentalists to participate in work vacations. Earthwatch is an international nonprofit organization that welcomes paying volunteers to work alongside scientists as they collect research to support environmental education and promote sustainable living. From the glaciers of Alaska to the savannah of Zimbabwe, "everyday people" are joining expeditions and making important strides in conservation. Prices, durations, accommodations, and activity levels vary greatly, with some trips costing as much as a conventional luxury vacation. There are specific suggested trips for families who want to travel and learn together, as well as recommended teen expeditions where young adults will have hands-on responsibilities, but with supervision and support. To explore their options, visit www.earthwatch.org.

The Sierra Club also offers volunteer tourism packages throughout the world. Knowing that the financial obligation of these exciting adventures can be a hardship for families, they have established the Sharon Churchwell Fund, which helps alleviate the cost of volunteer trips for 18- to 25-year-olds, and the Morley Fund, which sponsors educators who would not otherwise be able to afford such a trip. To find out how you can become a part of these trips, or to help others participate in making their eco-tourism dreams come true, visit www. sierraclub.org/outings.

If you love the idea of traveling, but a cross-country trip seems financially impossible, WWOOF USA could be your ticket to continental adventure. World-Wide Opportunities on Organic Farms—USA links volunteers with organic farmers. For a yearly membership of $20 to $30, you can contact organic farms throughout the country that will provide food and lodging in exchange for daily hours of cooperative farmwork. The website allows you to browse registered farms' requirements and accommodations, see whether children are welcome, and learn what points of interest are nearby. To contact the farms, you must pay for the directory. Get your hands dirty across the U.S.A. at www.wwoofusa.org. For those who prefer to travel to more exotic locations, contact the International WWOOF Association (www.wwoofinternational.org) and see which coop-farming opportunities are available abroad.

Planning a long-distance trip often involves taking an airplane, which uses fuel made from nonrenewable resources that release carbon dioxide and other toxins into the atmosphere. If you're going to be flying or driving for an extended amount of time, visit a site like www.terrapass.com to measure the environmental impact your trip will have using a carbon calculator. You can then explore carbon-offsetting options, like helping to fund energy-efficiency projects through industrial wind farms, to help remedy your output. Once you return home, up your eco-efforts by making this the spring you grow a family vegetable garden, help the children expand their recycling efforts to include mixed paper, or allot yourselves plenty of time to make holiday presents. Traveling is a terrific opportunity to see the wonders of our world; being mindful of our travel's impact helps ensure that those wonders remain exactly that.

Five-Minute Makeover

Is carbon offsetting the perfect answer to global warming? No. Since trees don't grow overnight, planting a dozen trees today won't erase yesterday's carbon-emitting flight. The concept of buying back carbon emissions is still a new one and, again, lends itself to a skewed belief that we can do whatever we want and then throw money at the problem. The best idea for any kind of travel is to do so responsibly and mindfully. Plan the most effective route for your trip, take time to pack the essentials so you won't have to buy more stuff on your trip, and remember your good green manners on the road.

Once you know where you're going, you'll want to make reservations in an establishment that's mindful of its environmental impact. Before you book your hotel, ask about the business's code of green conduct. Many hotels encourage patrons to reuse towels and bedding, have room keys that deactivate the lights and heating or cooling units when the room is unoccupied, and have recycling containers in the dining area. If these practices aren't posted, you can still do your part. Children can hang towels to dry, turn off all energy sources before leaving the room, and reuse recyclable containers until they can be disposed of properly. Reuse plastic water bottles from home to carry shampoo and conditioner, take short showers, and write a note to the management suggesting some of the simple green ideas you have implemented at home.

Once you arrive at your destination, you can continue to make greener choices. Opt for public transportation and see more of the area for less money, or rent a bike and incorporate exercise into your itinerary. If you have to rent a car, choose the smallest, most fuel-efficient vehicle for your needs. If possible, you might want to rent a hybrid for your trip and test-drive a different kind of car for a potential future purchase. Frequent neighborhood-owned businesses and restaurants, and sample local fare. Resist buying plastic souvenirs and trinkets, many of which are made elsewhere, and instead take digital pictures or save ticket stubs from museum visits. Help your children mail home postcards describing in detail the sights and sounds they're experiencing, or, if they aren't old enough to write themselves, trace their hands on the back of a letter they dictate to you before dropping it in the mailbox. When you get home, you'll have a personalized, time-stamped keepsake of your travels.

Whether you choose to visit another state or another country, it's important that your family make a commitment to be on their best green behavior. In my own travels, it always upsets me when I see fellow tourists disregarding well-marked trails to pick a wildflower or throwing rocks at wildlife to "wake them up for a good picture." As an eco-friendly family, it's important to remember that even when we're on vacation, we're still at home, on our planet. A big part of eco-friendly living is acknowledging and embracing that we're a global community. Wildflowers or wild animals, all people, places, and things deserve our environmental respect. Vacation is a time to relax your mind, not your ideals. Throw away your litter, look for recycling receptacles, and try to leave a tourist spot as beautiful as you found it.

Five-Minute Makeover

If you're traveling abroad, make an effort to learn to say "please" and "thank-you" in a foreign language. This small effort will be well received. When we make an effort to connect with other people, we're fostering our community-building ideals, making the world a kinder, more welcoming place to be. Keep in mind, too, that a warm smile costs nothing, means everything, and translates in any language.

Family Fun-Raisers

If you want to commemorate a special occasion while drawing attention to a cause close to your heart, try organizing a family fundraiser. With so many worthy causes needing attention, banding together as a family and enlisting the help of friends and neighbors is a great way to support a worthwhile cause, help your children appreciate the importance of charitable donations, and enjoy the camaraderie that naturally occurs when like-minded people work together toward a common goal. Children of all ages quickly learn that it takes money to fund projects. From Girl Scout cookie sales to high school yearbook car washes, fund-raising is a constant on the adolescent landscape. Greening that landscape is a great way to implement the ideals of reduce, reuse, recycle that your family is making a part of their lives while continuing to help others.

When people, especially children, learn that a problem exists, it's natural to want to help. For instance, after learning that sea turtles are being killed because they're accidentally ingesting plastic, your child may feel compelled to help these creatures. The World Wildlife Fund sponsors wildlife adoptions at its site, www.worldwildlife.org; monetary donations go directly to helping the animal of your choice—in this case, the sea turtle. Official certificates document your donation of $25, with plush sea turtle toys, a framed gift certificate, and a WWF map being given for donations of $250. Your donation goal is up to you, with gift incentives helping to inspire your young do-gooders to do more good.

Once you decide on which cause you'd like to support, you'll need to plan how to most effectively raise awareness and money for your chosen organization. For green purposes, solicit the help of as many people as you can in your 3R campaign. Many fund-raisers ask people to buy new products, with a percentage of the proceeds going toward the monetary goal. But a more eco-friendly alternative is to organize a fund-raiser that reduces, reuses, and recycles what we already have on hand. Hosting a silent auction can make this happen.

In a silent auction, donated items are attractively arranged around a table, each with a sheet describing the product and a starting bid price. Guests move around the room increasing the bid by filling in their name and the amount they are willing to pay. After a predeter-mined time, the bids are collected and the winners are announced. Of course, since our aim is to increase eco-awareness, you can tweak your event to be a "green" silent auction and auction off reusable and recycled goods, donating the profits to the cause of your choice.

Organization and presentation are critical to this event's success. Decide on the date and time, and who you'll invite. If you're joining forces with another family or organization, be sure to coordinate your calendars. For a family event, a Sunday afternoon that's conve-nient for extended family could work well, whereas an after-school club may prefer to have it on the same weeknight regular meetings take place. You should also plan to serve simple refreshments, like pitchers of water, coffee or tea, and homemade muffins.

A week before the event, you'll want everyone to collect the items that will be auctioned off. These could be gently used toys, pic-ture frames that no longer match the home's decor, clothes in good condition, CDs, DVDs, and presents that you've received but will never use. Once you have supplies on hand, make sure everything is cleaned, ironed, and working. CDs should be free of scratches, and electronic toys should have the batteries recharged to make the items even more enticing.

Next, arrange the items in an attractive manner for the auction. This isn't a garage sale, but an auction, where you want attendees to donate generously. A pile of winter clothes in the corner of a room is much less attractive than a coordinating scarf, hat, and mittens set in a basket next to snow toys. Take time to consider a fun name for the basket of goodies. In this instance, "Winter Wonderland Fun" could work. You can use baskets and boxes from around your home to put together various themed displays. Depending on the anticipated number of participants and guests, you could have anywhere from 10 to 30 baskets to bid on.

Once the baskets and boxes are ready, you'll want to decide what each one is worth. This is an excellent way to help children appreciate value. Working together, discuss the value of each item, reinforcing that even though most of these items aren't new, they've been well cared for and can be enjoyed by others. When they're cleaned, ironed, and polished, families can see that their effort can help breathe new life into an old item. Using recycled paper, note the intention of your auction, the basket's theme, its value, bidding increment increase values, and a suggested starting bid. Place information cards next to each basket with a pen, and arrange them on tables throughout the room.

As guests arrive, have children talk with them about their goals for the day. Open up the auction floor for a specific amount of time, serve refreshments, and then ask participants to place their final bids. Collect the bidding papers, announce the winners, and distribute the baskets. Collect your fund-raising dollars and thank everyone for coming. Be sure to save the bidding sheets so the children can specifically thank generous donors in their thank-you cards.

A family fund-raising project like this achieves its best success when everyone has a part in organizing and facilitating an event that's well grounded in eco-ideals and whose outcome benefits the household and the world at large. Big family projects like green silent auctions can also expose other people to meaningful eco-friendly activities, opening up a dialogue about the important changes we can all make in our homes to benefit our global community. Attracting others to our eco-friendly ways is yet another reward of greener living.

As you take the next step in greening your eco-friendly family, I remind you to enjoy the process and each other along the way. The suggestions and activities in this book have been designed with the whole family in mind. From guiding a toddler's first green steps to greening a teen's trendy lifestyle, you can inspire your family to see going green as a way of life that evolves, not just a to-do check-list that ends. Together you can all take eco-actions that help the planet, save money, and preserve energy while making memories whose effects extend far beyond your own backyard. By appealing to children early in life, we help ensure that the next generation will become conscientious consumers, passionate naturalists, and respon-sible conservationists who are personal advocates for Earth. Today is the day to change the world—one eco-friendly activity at a time.

Chapter Checklist

- ☐ We will look to personalize gifts for a guest of honor instead of relying solely on store-bought presents.

- ☐ We will approach celebrations from a greener perspective, look-ing for less wasteful ways of entertaining.

- ☐ We will continue to practice making good green choices, even when on vacation.

- ☐ We will invite friends and family to experience the social and ecological benefits of green fund-raising.

- ☐ We will continue to take responsibility for our local and global community through eco-friendly living.

Green Sites

While working on this book I was thrilled to find so many resources on going green. The sites compiled here represent some of the most up-to-date, practical, and meaningful information available on sustainable living. All of the products recommended are committed to environmentally responsible practices and whenever possible, have been personally tested. It is my hope that *Eco-Friendly Families* will inspire you to continue walking a greener path. These sources can help you do just that.

Eco-Friendly Websites

These professional websites are loaded with interesting links, articles, and the latest green facts and figures, putting even more green ideas right at your fingertips.

U.S. Environmental Protection Agency   **www.epa.gov**
Government department dedicated to safe and healthy living.

Earth Easy   **www.eartheasy.com**
Ideas for environmentally sustainable living, with a focus on simplifying.

Healthy Child, Healthy World   **www.healthychild.org**
The five easy steps in the Blue Butterfly Campaign can help protect the health and well-being of children from harmful environmental exposures.

Green Guide   www.thegreenguide.com
National Geographic's comprehensive website and bimonthly
newsletter that offers practical advice on how to lead a more
environmentally sensitive life.

LIME Radio—Sirius
Satellite Channel 114   www.sirius.com/siriusinternetradio
A whole channel devoted to living a more balanced lifestyle.

Mothering magazine   www.mothering.com
A family-living magazine addressing contemporary health,
environmental, and lifestyle issues in an upbeat, intelligent,
compassionate, and courageous way.

Tree Hugger   www.treehugger.com
A one-stop shop for green news, solutions, and product information that is helping to drive sustainability mainstream.

Reduce, Reuse, Recycle

These websites can help you take green action that lightens your load
without weighing down the environment.

American Council for
Energy Efficient Economy   www.greenercars.org
Rates all cars for environmental efficiency and organizes findings based on model and class.

Apple   www.apple.com/environment
Online trade-in options for working electronics, like desktops,
camcorders, and game systems.

Best Buy   www.bestbuy.com
If you are upgrading models, Best Buy will take away your old
television when delivering your new one.

Circuit City   www.cc.eztradein.com
Online trade-in options for working electronics, like desktops,
camcorders, and game systems.

Cox Target Media   www.coxtarget.com
Remove yourself from Valpak Savings' mailing list.

Dress for Success   www.dressforsuccess.org
A nonprofit organization committed to helping disadvantaged women suit up for a job interview.

E-Cycling Central   www.eiea.com
Contact electronic donation programs across the country.

Earth 911   www.earth911.org
A leading environmental resource that can help you find local ways to recycle everything.

Filter for Good   www.filterforgood.com
The advantages of drinking tap water over bottled water.

The Glass Slipper Project   www.glassslipperproject.org
Donate formalwear for prom.

Goodwill   www.goodwill.org
Donate furniture and appliances.

Greendisk   www.greendisk.com
This company will reuse or recycle all of your "technotrash."

Hewlett Packard   www.hp.com/united-states/tradein
Online trade-in options for working electronics like desktops, camcorders, and game systems.

Kidzsignments   www.kidzsignments.com
Twice-yearly consignment sales.

Making Memories   www.makingmemories.org
Donate your wedding gown to help raise money for breast cancer patients and their families.

Materials for the Arts   www.mfta.com
Reuses materials to help community programs and nonprofits expand.

Nike's Reuse-A-Shoe Program   www.nike.com/nikebiz
Accepts all brands of athletic shoes and grinds them up to use for new sports surfaces, like basketball courts.

Optoutpresceen.com   www.optoutprescreen.com
Opt out of credit and insurance offers sent by the three major reporting companies.

The Princess Project   www.princessproject.org
Donate formal wear for prom.

Project Smile   www.projectsmile.com
Collects like-new stuffed animals that firefighters and police
officers can distribute to children during a traumatic time.

Recycline   www.recycline.com
Company that manufactures personal-care products like toothbrushes and razors using 100 percent recycled material for plastic handles.

Refill not Landfill   www.refillnotlandfill.com
An online campaign to reduce disposable water bottle waste.

Reusable Bags   www.reusablebags.com
A huge selection of reusable bags and other sustainable products.

Soles4Soles   www.soles4souls.com
Accepts gently worn shoes and delivers them to people in need.

Tools for Schools   www.toolsforschoolssolutions.org
Redistributes everything from office chairs to artwork, to help
public schools grow.

Verizon   www.verizon.com
Recycles obsolete rechargeable batteries.

Plant, Grow, Eat

Learn more about how to cultivate a healthy diet with these food-
focused sites.

Biodynamics   www.biodynamics.com
Biodynamic Farming and Gardening Association.

Community Supported
Garden at Genesis Farm   www.csgatgenesisfarm.com
Learn more about the important work of community-supported
gardens, and find one in your area.

Compost Guide   www.compostguide.com
Everything you need to know about starting a home composting practice.

Environmental Working Group   www.foodnews.org
Research and advocacy group that compiled the "dirty dozen" of produce.

Kids Gardening   www.kidsgardening.org
A division of the National Gardening Association specifically targeting young gardeners.

Super Baby Foods   www.superbabyfoods.com
Ruth Yaron's comprehensive book on making your own baby food, from introducing solids to healthy toddler snacks.

Super Foods   www.deliaquigley.com
A comprehensive guide to the best seasonal eating options.

Whole Foods Market   www.wholefoodsmarket.com
World's leading retailer of natural and organic foods.

Sustainable Products

Be a more conscious consumer with the help of these eco-minded organizations.

Eco By Design   www.ecobydesign.com
Offers a natural wool carpeting system that is not contaminated with chemicals.

The Energy Star   www.energystar.gov
The Star criterion includes awarding products that use 10 to 50 percent less energy than is federally mandated.

Gdiapers   www.gdiapers.com
Hybrid diaper combining sustainable cloth and disposable inserts.

Green Elements Design   www.greenelementsdesign.com
Sustainable nontoxic design and building supplies for homeowners, designers, contractors, and builders.

Hobbs Bonded Fibers   www.hobbsbondedfibers.com/quilters
The Hobbs Heirloom Organics Batting is 100 percent organic craft cotton.

Klean Kanteen   www.kleankanteen.com
A 100 percent stainless-steel thermos that is dishwasher safe and nontoxic, and holds hot or cold beverages.

Laptop Lunch   www.laptoplunches.com
A fashionable, eco-friendly lunchbox that is reusable, recyclable, and dishwasher safe.

A Natural Home   www.anaturalhome.com
Organic pillows, bedding, and home accessories.

Natural Home Products   www.naturalhomeproducts.com
Carpeting options that will have everyone in your family breathing easier.

Sigg   www.mysigg.com
Sports bottles made from a single piece of aluminum. These bottles are spill proof, leak proof, and 100% recyclable.

Think Baby   www.thinkbabybottles.com
Bottles made without potentially leaching plastics or lead.

Under the Canopy   www.underthecanopy.com
Organic pillows, bedding, and home accessories.

Wrap-N-Mat   www.wrap-n-mat.com
Washable sandwich wrap that opens to a lunch mat.

Commercial Cleaning Products

Browse these sites to find safer ways to keep your home and the earth clean.

Biokleen   www.biokleenhome.com
Natural, nontoxic cleaning products for home and office.

Mrs. Meyers   www.mrsmeyers.com
Laundry, pet, and home-cleaning products made with essential oils.

Seventh Generation   www.seventhgeneration.com
Healthy and safe household and personal-care products.

Shaklee   www.shaklee.net
Nontoxic products that have been trusted for over 50 years.

Greener Gift Giving

Celebrate special occasions in eco-style with presents that help take care of the future.

Amazon   www.amazon.com
> Shop for reused books or consolidate your shipping with this one-stop online megastore.

Acorn   www.acornplace.com
> Natural parenting and green living items for the whole family.

Arbonne International   www.andreatriche.myarbonne.com
> Botanically based skin care formulated without dyes or chemical fragrances.

Blessed Nest   www.blessednest.com
> Sustainable and practical presents that are handmade in the United States under fair and favorable working conditions.

Global Exchange   www.globalexchange.com
> Leading online distributor of certified Fair Trade products.

Heifer International   www.heifer.org
> Gifts that help families around the world learn how to become self-sustaining.

Kiddie Cradles   www.kiddiecradles.com
> Baby carriers made with fabric from recycled wood pulp (tencel) and recycled plastic bottles (fleece).

Little Willow Baby   www.littlewillowbaby.com
> Wide selection of cloth diaper options and other simple, natural products.

Tread Earth Lightly   www.treadearthlightly.com
> Organic, sustainable, and chemical-free products for the whole family.

Eco-Tourism

Travel responsibly and enhance your experiences and the environment at the same time.

Earthwatch   www.earthwatch.org
> International nonprofit organization that welcomes paying volunteers to work alongside scientists throughout the world.

The Sierra Club   www.sierraclub.org/outings
> Offers volunteer tourism packages throughout the world.

Terra Pass   www.terrapass.com
> Carbon calculator, to measure the environmental impact your trip will have, and carbon-offsetting options.

World of WWOOF   www.wwoofinternational.org
> Cooperative farming opportunities throughout the world.

**The World-Wide Opportunities
on Organic Farms—USA**   www.wwoofusa.org
> Cooperative farming opportunities throughout the United States.

The World Wildlife Fund   www.worldwildlife.org
> Sponsors wildlife adoptions to protect endangered species.